DISC W9-AHH-490

Hartland Public Library
P.O. Box 137
Hartland, VT 05048-0137

Mormons in America

Religion in American Life

JON BUTLER & HARRY S. STOUT
GENERAL EDITORS

Mormons in America

*Claudia Lauper Bushman
and Richard Lyman Bushman*

OXFORD UNIVERSITY PRESS
New York • Oxford

To our grandchildren, who will soon be old enough to read this book.

Oxford University Press

Oxford New York
Athens Auckland Bangkok Bogotá Buenos Aires Calcutta
Cape Town Chennai Dar es Salaam Delhi Florence Hong Kong Istanbul
Karachi Kuala Lumpur Madrid Melbourne Mexico City Mumbai
Nairobi Paris São Paulo Singapore Taipei Tokyo Toronto Warsaw

and associated companies in
Berlin Ibadan

Copyright © 1999 by Claudia L. Bushman and Richard L. Bushman

Published by Oxford University Press, Inc.
198 Madison Avenue, New York, New York 10016

Oxford is a registered trademark of Oxford University Press

All rights reserved. No part of this publication
may be reproduced, stored in a retrieval system, or transmitted,
in any form or by any means, electronic, mechanical,
photocopying, recording, or otherwise, without the prior
permission of Oxford University Press.

Bushman, Claudia L.
    Mormons in America / Claudia L. Bushman and Richard L. Bushman.
        p. cm. — (Religion in American life)
    Includes bibliographical references and index.
    1. Mormon Church—United States—Juvenile literature. 2. Church
of Jesus Christ of Latter-day Saints—Juvenile literature.
    [1. Mormon Church. 2. Church of Jesus Christ of Latter-day Saints.]
    I. Bushman, Richard L. II. Title. III. Series
BX8635.2.B85   1998
289.3'73—dc21   98-18605
                        CIP
                          AC

ISBN 0-19-510677-6 (library edition)

9 8 7 6 5 4 3 2 1

Printed in the United States of America
on acid-free paper

Design and layout: Loraine Machlin
Picture research: Lisa Kirchner

On the cover: A quilt, *Come Let Us Rejoice*, by Charlotte Andersen
Frontispiece: A modern Mormon family gathers around the table for discussion

Contents

Introduction 7

Jon Butler & Harry S. Stout

CHAPTER 1

Joseph Smith's First Visions, 1820–30 11

CHAPTER 2

Zion, 1831–37 25

CHAPTER 3

Nauvoo, 1838–46 39

CHAPTER 4

The Westward Trek, 1846–69 57

CHAPTER 5

Building the Kingdom, 1847–69 69

CHAPTER 6

Mormon Women, 1831–90 81

CHAPTER 7

Mormons in the Nation, 1890–1945 99

CHAPTER 8

The Church Since 1945 113

Chronology 132

Further Reading 136

Index 140

Introduction

JON BUTLER & HARRY S. STOUT, GENERAL EDITORS

The history of the Mormons—the Church of Jesus Christ of Latter-day Saints—is a unique, fascinating, and immensely important story that illustrates religion's dramatic importance in American history. The Mormon movement emerged in upstate New York after Joseph Smith, the Mormon prophet, found golden tablets from which he translated the Book of Mormon, the Mormon's principal modern revelation, published by Smith in March of 1830. The movement grew rapidly, aided by the religious turmoil common throughout antebellum America. Mormonism prospered despite numerous setbacks including the assassination of Joseph Smith in 1844; the dangerous migration to Utah led by Smith's successor, Brigham Young; open warfare with the United States government; and federal legislation outlawing polygamy or "plural marriage" (which Mormons officially abandoned in 1890). At the end of the twentieth century Mormonism remains one of the world's fastest growing religions, with its several million members seeking ever more converts in virtually every country where religious freedom is practiced.

The history of the Church of Jesus Christ of Latter-day Saints described here by Claudia and Richard Bushman reflects religion's dynamic character in American society and history. The Bushmans explain Josephs Smith's distinctive role in a society well known for reli-

The Mormon Tabernacle Choir, in the Tabernacle on Temple Square in Salt Lake City, Utah.

gious innovation. They explain how Smith deftly built a formidable institutional apparatus to manage increasingly complex church affairs. They demonstrate the unique role women played in Mormon affairs, both before and after the Mormons' practice of polygamy. They reveal how the Utah migration transformed Mormonism while retaining unique beliefs and practices dating back to the earliest years of Mormon activity. They explain how Mormonism addressed the challenges of modernity and how this nineteenth-century religion made an indelible impact on modern America and, indeed, in the world. Throughout, the Bushmans demonstrate how the rise of a small and persecuted movement intersected and even transformed the history of the American nation.

This book is part of a unique 17-volume series that explores the evolution, character, and dynamics of religion in American life from 1500 to the end of the 20th century. It is impossible to capture the flavor and character of the American experience without understanding the connections between secular activities and religion. Spirituality stood at the center of Native American societies before European colonization and has continued to do so long after. Religion—and the freedom to express it—motivated milllions of immigrants to come to America from remarkably different cultures, and the exposure to new ideas and ways of living shaped their experience. It also fueled tension among different ethnic and racial groups in America and, regretfully, accounted for difficult episodes of bigotry in American society. Religion urged Americans to expand the nation—first within the continental United States, then through overseas conquests and missionary work—and has had a profound influence on American politics, from the era of the Puritans to the present. Finally, religion contributes to the extraordinary diversity that has, for four centuries, made the United States one of the world's most dynamic societies.

The Religion in American Life series explores the historical traditions that have made religious freedom and spiritual exploration central features of American society. It emphasizes the experience of religion in America—what men and women have understood by religion, how it has affected politics and society, and how Americans have used it to shape their daily lives.

Religion in American Life

JON BUTLER & HARRY S. STOUT
GENERAL EDITORS

RELIGION IN COLONIAL AMERICA
Jon Butler

RELIGION IN NINETEENTH CENTURY AMERICA
Grant Wacker

RELIGION IN TWENTIETH CENTURY AMERICA
Randall Balmer

CATHOLICS IN AMERICA
James T. Fisher

PROTESTANTS IN AMERICA
Mark Noll

ORTHODOX CHRISTIANS IN AMERICA
John A. Erickson

JEWS IN AMERICA
Hasia Diner

MUSLIMS IN AMERICA
Frederick Denny

NATIVE AMERICAN RELIGION
Joel W. Martin

MORMONS IN AMERICA
Claudia Lauper Bushman & Richard Lyman Bushman

BUDDHISTS, HINDUS, AND SIKHS IN AMERICA
Gurinder Singh Mann, Paul Numrich, & Raymond B. Williams

ALTERNATIVE RELIGIOUS TRADITIONS IN AMERICA
Stephen J. Stein

CHURCH AND STATE IN AMERICA
Edwin S. Gaustad

IMMIGRATION AND AMERICAN RELIGION
Jenna Weissman Joselit

WOMEN AND AMERICAN RELIGION
Ann Braude

AFRICAN-AMERICAN RELIGION
Albert J. Raboteau

BIOGRAPHICAL SUPPLEMENT AND SERIES INDEX
Darryl Hart and Ann Henderson Hart

Chapter 1

Joseph Smith's First Visions, 1820–30

While I was thus in the act of calling upon God, I discovered a light appearing in my room, which continued to increase until the room was lighter than at noonday, when immediately a personage appeared at my bedside, standing in the air, for his feet did not touch the floor.

— Joseph Smith, Jr., *"History," Papers of Joseph Smith*, Volume 1, 1839

Mormonism, one of the world's fastest-growing Christian religions, doubles its membership about every 15 years. The Church of Jesus Christ of Latter-day Saints (the formal name of the Mormon church) now claims more than 10 million members, more than half of whom are outside the United States. Within a decade after its organization in New York State in 1830 the church had more than twenty thousand adherents, and it has grown rapidly ever since.

Mormonism is a Christian denomination. Mormons believe in the Bible as other Christians do and accept most traditional Christian doctrines regarding faith in Christ, the need for repentance, and the importance of loving one's neighbor. Joseph Smith, the faith's first "prophet" or spiritual leader, said his intention was to restore the true religion of the Bible, not start something entirely new. But Mormonism is a Christian religion with a difference. Smith did not follow the path of earlier Protestant reformers, like Martin Luther or John Calvin, learned men

Joseph Smith, the first prophet and founder of the Church of Jesus Christ of Latter-day Saints. Because no photograph was ever taken of Smith, depictions are based on written descriptions and a mold of his face made upon his death.

who reasoned their way to new interpretations of the Bible. Smith, born December 23, 1805 in Sharon, Vermont, and brought up on farms in Vermont and New York had little schooling as a boy and rarely attended church. Nothing prepared him to debate with the educated clergy as Luther and Calvin did. Smith did not search the Bible for new insights or find fault with the teachings of other churches as the starting point for his religion. He said he received his doctrines directly from heaven like prophets of ancient times. Angels appeared to him and the Holy Spirit inspired his mind. He made a fresh beginning by communicating directly with God.

Because of the heavenly revelations he is believed to have received, Joseph Smith has the same place in Mormon history as Moses does in the history of the Jews. Mormons honor Smith as a prophet who taught the law of God and led his people. In Jewish tradition Moses recorded his revelations in the first five books of the Bible. Joseph Smith's revelations have been compiled into a work called the *Doctrine and Covenants*, a book of scripture for Mormons that supplements the Old and New Testaments. In short, Mormons think of Joseph Smith as a prophet very much like those who wrote the Bible.

Smith's revelations began when he was a boy, in answer to a prayer for guidance. He was then living in New York near a little town called Palmyra, bordering the route of the Erie Canal, which was under construction at the time. In that period there were many preachers who were seeking to convince people that they had sinned and must depend on Christ to save them. Joseph Smith, although not overly religious until then, worried about his worthiness and wanted assurance of God's forgiveness. But the diversity of churches confused him. Four churches met in the village of Palmyra—the Methodists, Presbyterians, Baptists, and Quakers—all with slightly varying doctrines. Joseph Smith did not know whom to trust or which church to attend, making it difficult for him to find answers to his religious questions.

His parents, Joseph Smith, Sr., and Lucy Mack Smith, could not give him much help. They had drifted away from the Congregational church in New England at a time when the old religions were breaking up and

Unable to determine for himself what church or sect was right, 14-year-old Joseph Smith asked God, "If any of them be right, which is it?" God's answer came amidst a pillar of light.

splintering into scores of different churches. Preachers and visionaries confused worshipers with their own versions of Christianity, making it hard to know where the truth lay. And the movement of the population from country to city as well as east to west hastened the disruption of traditional churches. In this flow of migrants, Joseph Smith's grandparents, for example, had moved from settled towns in Massachusetts and Connecticut to Vermont, leaving behind their ancestors' religion.

Although Smith's parents were believing Christians, the family rarely attended church. As tenant farmers who rented land for most of their married life—Joseph was born on a rented farm in Vermont—they never settled anywhere long enough to join a local church. When the Smiths moved from Vermont to Palmyra in 1816 and became able to buy a farm, his mother attended the Presbyterian Church, but his father refused to go with her, believing that the churches were full of hypocrites. This family division added to young Joseph's confusion.

Smith's religious concern climaxed in 1820 when he was 14. He later wrote that he was "excedingly distressed for I become convicted of my sins and by searching the scriptures I found that mankind did not come unto the Lord but that they had apostatised [fallen away] from the true and liveing faith." Hoping to find the truth for himself, he went to pray in the woods near his father's clearing. To his amazement, as he prayed, "A piller of light above the brightness of the sun at noon day come down from above and rested upon me and I was filled with the spirit of god and the Lord opened the heavens upon me and I saw the Lord and he spake unto me saying Joseph my son thy sins are forgiven thee." Grateful for God's mercy, Smith also asked which church he should join. The being that he called the Lord told him not to join any: "They have turned asside from the gospel and keep not my commandments."

When Smith told a minister about his visions, the man was suspicious. He said that "all such things had ceased with the Apostles and there never would be any more of them." The minister pressured the boy to deny his experiences, but he refused. Although he was poorly educated, as the spelling and grammatical errors in his account reveal, he relied on the messages from heaven and his own understanding of God's will.

The vision did not immediately transform Smith's life. Over the next few years, he said, "I fell into transgression and sinned in many things which brought a wound upon my soul." But his religious experiences were not at an end. He prayed again for forgiveness in 1823, when he was seventeen, and received a revelation then that was more extraordinary than the first. Once again a heavenly person appeared. An angel calling himself Moroni told Smith about "plates of gold" containing an account of people who had lived centuries earlier on the North American continent. Smith learned that he was to translate the characters on the plates, creating a work that came to be known as the Book of Mormon.

The 1823 vision included a view of the gold plates: thin metal sheets inscribed with ancient writing, bound together by large rings. The next day Smith went to the location he had seen in the vision, pried up a rock, and saw the plates lying in a stone box. But when he tried to lift them out, he suffered a shock that stopped him short. After three attempts, the angel Moroni returned and told him he could not have the plates yet. Smith had earlier been cautioned against trying to become rich from the plates, but coming up the hill he "had been tempted of the advisary [by an adversary] and saught the Plates to obtain riches and kept not the commandment that I should have an eye single to the glory of God." A poor young man whose family was trying to pay off the mortgage on their farm might well be tempted by the thought of potential riches, but even thinking of them delayed the recovery of the plates for four years. Not until 1827 did Smith receive them and begin translation of the text.

Moroni's visit occurred on September 22, 1823. From then on Joseph Smith had revelations and visions to the end of his life. These stories of revelations seem strange in an age when accounts of the supernatural are discounted. Even believing Christians, who accept biblical revelations, distrust a modern visionary, especially one as poor and uneducated as Joseph Smith. To explain his visions, critics have suggested various explanations. Smith's contemporaries thought he was a fraud who made up stories to deceive his followers. A noted twentieth-century biographer called him a great fabricator with a gift for making up stories who was carried along by his own success. Others have offered psychological explanations related to epileptic seizures or "automatic" writing coming uninvited from his subconscious mind. Most recently, people have suspended judgment, granting that religious experiences may be authentic for those who undergo them but not necessarily be real in a scientific sense. One recent commentator, an avowed atheist, called Joseph Smith a religious genius.

Unfazed by general disbelief, Mormons consider the Joseph Smith revelation stories to be actual events when God spoke to people on earth. Moroni's appearance to Smith in 1823 and the 1820 visit of the Lord to

Emma Hale Smith married Joseph Smith against her father's wishes. For a short time she helped translate the Book of Mormon.

him seem credible to Mormons. Joseph Smith's simple narrative of the events, his naive and untutored language describing them, and the concrete details in the accounts make the stories convincing. Most important, Mormons feel they are themselves in touch with God through these occurrences. They say that anyone who sincerely asks God for inspiration will believe them too. It is their faith in these founding stories that sets the Mormons apart from other Christians.

At first only Joseph Smith's family believed his stories. His father, a visionary himself, accepted his son's account without hesitation. He believed in buried treasure, which he tried to find with the help of magic rituals, a practice common among rural Yankees. An angel guarding a pile of gold plates seemed possible to him, as magic and religion blended in the family culture. But the warnings of Moroni showed Joseph that he had to put aside magical pursuits to make room for a religious mission.

During those years from 1823 to 1827, Joseph and his father went on a treasure-hunting expedition near Harmony, Pennsylvania, just south of the New York state line. By this time Joseph had become reluctant to look for treasure and went along only at his father's insistence, because the family needed the money. The expedition yielded no treasure, but Joseph met an attractive young woman in the household where he and his father boarded. He told his mother that tall, dark-haired Emma Hale "would be my choice in preference to any other woman I have ever seen." Isaac Hale, Emma's father, did not want his daughter to marry a poor treasure hunter. But Emma liked the tall, handsome Joseph, with his broad chest, light brown hair, and long-lashed blue eyes. "Preferring to marry him to any other man I knew," she later told her son, Joseph III, she married Smith in January 1827, against her father's wishes.

Joseph and Emma Smith were devoted to each other. When she lay near death after the birth of their first child, he nursed her back to health.

She eventually bore nine children, only four of whom lived to maturity. One of Smith's revelations spoke of her religious mission: "Thy time shall be given to writing, and to learning much." She produced the first Mormon hymn book and led the church's women's organization, the Relief Society.

In September 1827, Joseph and Emma Smith were back at his family's farm near Palmyra. The time had come to retrieve the plates. Shortly after midnight on September 22, the two rode to the hill where the gold plates were buried and Joseph removed them. With the plates, Smith said, was a pair of unusual eyeglasses for interpreting them. Two stones set in rims were attached to a breastplate worn over the shoulders. Smith was told that if he looked through the stones he would be able to translate the engravings on the plates.

After recovering the plates, Joseph and Emma moved to Harmony, Pennsylvania. Emma's forgiving father supplied them with a small cabin and a few acres of land, and Smith began to translate the characters, which were like the ancient Egyptian hieroglyphic picture script. (A sample of these characters still exists.) Writing and translating an unfamiliar narrative posed problems for a young man whose wife later said that in 1829 he could not even write a decent letter. Yet those who saw him at work said that he looked into the interpreting device and read out the words with no hesitation. When he picked up after a break, he did not review the last translated passage but went straight on. His words were taken down by someone else sitting in the room, Emma at first but then others who wanted to be part of

Title page of the first LDS hymnal, compiled by Emma Hale Smith and published in 1835.

A COLLECTION

OF

SACRED HYMNS,

FOR THE

CHURCH

OF THE

LATTER DAY SAINTS.

SELECTED BY EMMA SMITH.

Kirtland, Ohio:

Printed by F. G. Williams & co.

: : : : : : : : :

1835.

A page from the original Book of Mormon of 1830. Joseph Smith did not change or revise the text as he dictated. One of his scribes stated, "These were days never to be forgotten—to sit under the sound of a voice dictated by the inspiration of heaven."

THE

BOOK OF MORMON:

AN ACCOUNT WRITTEN BY THE HAND OF MOR-
MON, UPON PLATES TAKEN FROM
THE PLATES OF NEPHI.

Wherefore it is an abridgment of the Record of the People of Nephi; and also of the Lamanites; written to the Lamanites, which are a remnant of the House of Israel; and also to Jew and Gentile; written by way of commandment, and also by the spirit of Prophesy and of Revelation. Written, and sealed up, and hid up unto the Lord, that they might not be destroyed; to come forth by the gift and power of God unto the interpretation thereof; sealed by the hand of Moroni, and hid up unto the Lord, to come forth in due time by the way of Gentile; the interpretation thereof by the gift of God; an abridgment taken from the Book of Ether.

Also, which is a Record of the People of Jared, which were scattered at the time the Lord confounded the language of the people when they were building a tower to get to Heaven: which is to shew unto the remnant of the House of Israel how great things the Lord hath done for their fathers; and that they may know the covenants of the Lord, that they are not cast off forever; and also to the convincing of the Jew and Gentile that Jesus is the Christ, the Eternal God, manifesting Himself unto all nations. And now if there be fault, it be the mistake of men; wherefore condemn not the things of God, that ye may be found spotless at the judgment seat of Christ.

BY JOSEPH SMITH, JUNIOR,
AUTHOR AND PROPRIETOR.

PALMYRA:
PRINTED BY E. B. GRANDIN, FOR THE AUTHOR.
1830.

---

this unusual enterprise. Oliver Cowdery, a schoolteacher who heard about the gold plates from Smith's parents in Palmyra, arrived in Harmony in April 1829 and proved the most satisfactory scribe. From then on the Book of Mormon was written out in a great rush, first in Harmony and later at the house of another friendly family, the Whitmers, of Fayette, New York. By June 1829, three months after he and Oliver had begun in earnest, Joseph Smith applied for a copyright. He found a print-er in Palmyra and typesetting began in August 1829. In March 1830 the local newspaper announced the publication of the Book of Mormon.

The Book of Mormon purports to be the religious history of a civi-lization that once existed in Central America. Just as the Bible records the prophecies and history of the people of Israel in Palestine, the Book of Mormon contains revelations of a people in Central America. This histo-ry goes back thousands of years before the time of Christ and ends in 421 A.D., some fourteen hundred years before Joseph Smith's time.

The 531 pages in the current edition of the Book of Mormon contain hundreds of personalities, intricate stories of wars and battles, warnings and exhortations from prophets, complicated doctrinal expositions, and passages of religious devotion. It is not what you would expect from an uneducated Yankee farmer. Though presumably about the ancestors of the American Indians, the book says nothing of the stereotypical artifacts familiar to Americans of Joseph Smith's time, like canoes, wigwams, or peace pipes. All in all, the Book of Mormon is a remarkable production for an inexperienced young man who was just twenty-four when the book was published.

The Book of Mormon is like the Bible in many ways. The people in it emigrated from Jerusalem and were themselves Israelites. Leaving in 600 B.C., a few years before the Jews were taken into captivity in Babylon, they carried the writings of the Old Testament prophets with them. They stud-ied Isaiah and copied lengthy segments of his writings into the Book of Mormon. In a sense, the departure from Jerusalem in the Book of Mormon parallels Israel's exodus from Egypt to the Promised Land. The Book of Mormon exodus was much smaller, though, with only two fami-lies, probably no more than 50 people in all. They traveled down the Arabian peninsula to the sea, built a boat, and, driven by the wind, crossed the Indian and Pacific Oceans to America. Mormon scholars believe this small band landed on the west coast of Central America.

In their new land a rivalry between brothers—Nephi, a prophet and inspiring leader on the one side, and Laman and Lemuel, jealous older brothers on the other—developed into warring factions. The descendants of Laman and Lemuel, called Lamanites, attacked the followers of Nephi, the Nephites. Battles between these two nations raged down to the end of their history, when the Lamanites ultimately killed off the Nephites. Moroni, the last of his people the Nephites, finished the historical record and buried the gold plates Smith found in New York. (Mormons debate how the plates got there.)

Although alike in many ways, the Bible and the Book of Mormon differ in their writing style and the contents of the prophecies. The Book of Mormon is simpler to read; Nephi said that his soul delighted in plainness. No Book of Mormon prophets wrote poetry as complex as Isaiah's or recorded mystical visions as intricate and baffling as Ezekiel's. The Book of Mormon prophets spoke more directly about the Christ whose life had been foretold. People were warned to prepare for his coming.

At the climax of the book, Jesus appears to people in Central America. For generations they had anticipated this event. At Christ's death on the cross in Jerusalem and before His resurrection, terrible destruction came upon America—storms, earthquakes, a dark mist. These cataclysms destroyed the wicked, and only the righteous remained to see Christ when he descended from heaven as a resurrected person. He taught the people for many days, repeating the Sermon on the Mount, administering the Lord's supper, and foretelling coming events. After he ascended into heaven, the people lived together peacefully for two hundred years. Then wickedness and dissension divided the Lamanites and Nephites, and the two nations plunged once more into war. A Nephite general named Mormon led his nation into battle and rewrote the history of the two peoples, abbreviating and editing their accumulated records. It is for him that the Book of Mormon was named, and it was his son Moroni who buried the plates containing these records and later appeared as an angel to Joseph Smith.

As Joseph Smith began to distribute the Book of Mormon in March 1830, a few people started believing in the book and in him. One observed that it was "a book, a strange book, a very strange book." What could have appealed to these first readers? Some may have read the Book of Mormon as a history of Indian origins, a subject of speculation at that

time. Others may have appreciated its clarification of contested doctrines like baptism and the nature of Christ's redemption. For many, the book itself, coming from an uneducated young man, was evidence enough of God at work.

Joseph Smith said that after he completed his translation of the plates he returned them to the angel Moroni. Before he did, however, others also saw them. Their actual existence was thus not left entirely to conjecture. Although Smith was told not to show the plates to anyone while he was translating them, there were exceptions after he finished. In the front of the book appeared two statements signed by eleven witnesses who said they had seen the plates. Three witnesses signed a document reporting that "an angel of God came down from heaven, and he brought and laid

The Flight of Lehi and his people. They discovered the Liahona, a compass or director "prepared . . . by the hand of the Lord" for the Book of Mormon prophet Lehi, as he and his family traveled in the wilderness south of Jerusalem.

Joseph Smith copied these characters from gold plates that were revealed to him by the angel Moroni. Although recognizably Egyptian, the characters appear in a form that cannot be translated.

before our eyes, that we beheld and saw the plates." Eight other witnesses affirmed that "as many of the leaves as the said Smith has translated we did handle with our hands; and we also saw the engravings thereon." These statements may have reduced the skepticism of readers who wanted proof before believing themselves.

These eleven witnesses and their families came together with a handful of other believers soon after the publication of the Book of Mormon to organize a church. On April 6, 1830, about fifty people met in the Peter Whitmer cabin, in Fayette, New York, to accept Joseph Smith and Oliver Cowdery as their leaders. The two of them ordained each other as elders in the church, then prayed and preached. They had launched a new church.

Because the Book of Mormon told about the ancestors of the Native Americans, the early Mormons took an interest in the American West. In October 1830, four missionaries set off to visit Indian nations: first near Buffalo, New York, and Sandusky, Ohio, then on to the boundary of Indian country in western Missouri. These missionaries traveled 1,500 miles out, mostly by foot, presenting the Book of Mormon as a religious history of the Indians and a prophecy of their future part in God's plan.

They had little luck with the Indians, but on their way the missionaries made some significant converts. After leaving New York, the four stopped in Kirtland, Ohio, a small village east of Cleveland, where one of them knew an important local preacher named Sidney Rigdon. He and his congregation were seeking the pure religion of the New Testament and were interested in the missionaries' account of a new revelation. Within a few weeks many of them, including Rigdon himself, joined the Mormons, more than doubling the size of the church.

After the missionaries continued their journey west, Rigdon and a companion traveled back to New York to meet Joseph Smith. Rigdon, who was then the only member of the church with much education or literary ability, was warmly welcomed. A revelation called him to assist Smith, but reminded him that learning was not everything. "I call upon the weak things of the world, those who are unlearned, and despised, to thrash the nations by the power of my Spirit," the revelation said. The young prophet attracted many experienced men whom he pressed into service, but he yielded his leadership to none of them.

Shortly after Rigdon arrived in New York with the good news of the Kirtland converts, a revelation instructed Smith to move the entire church to Ohio. This revelation promised "a land flowing with milk and honey" and the bestowal of spiritual blessings. "There I will give unto you my law; and there you shall be endowed with power from on high." The original New York converts accordingly sold their farms and moved west, the first of many moves the Mormons would make over the coming years as they attempted to practice their religion without interference. Joseph and Emma Smith left New York for Ohio in January 1831, and the remainder of the church followed in the spring.

Chapter 2

Zion, 1831–37

And the Lord called his people Zion, because they were of one heart and one mind, and and dwelt in righteousness; and there was no poor among them.
—*Book of Moses,* 7:18

When the small band of Mormons straggled into Kirtland, Ohio, during the winter and spring of 1831, the new church was still largly undefined. The Book of Mormon, the church's most distinctive feature, provided no creed or program for action. Like the Bible, the Book of Mormon was a sprawling compilation of history, sermons, prophesies, and visions with no single, outstanding doctrine other than faith in Christ. Joseph Smith's revelations reaffirmed such basic Christian principles as repentance, but they only faintly outlined a special mission. The titles of church officers—elder, priest, teacher, and deacon—were familiar from Protestant churches, but the particular character of the new church was yet to be determined.

Within six months, Joseph Smith made a number of bold departures from traditional Protestantism. Less than two weeks after his arrival in Kirtland, he had a revelation "embracing the law of the Church" that laid out a new social and economic order in a specific location. Missionaries were to travel west until "it shall be revealed unto you from on high, when the city of the New Jerusalem shall be prepared, that ye may be gathered in one." In the Bible, the New Jerusalem was a heavenly city that

The courthouse and town square at Independence, Missouri, as it looked after the Mormons arrived and planned the town. Near were they planned to build a temple and found the new Jerusalem.

was to come to earth when Christ returned. In Smith's revelation, the saints were to construct a New Jerusalem on earth as the center of a godly society organized on divine principles.

According to this plan, the members of the New Jerusalem community were to divide their property among themselves to eliminate inequality, just as the New Testament Christians had held all things in common. The members of this community, called Saints, were to deed over everything they owned—land, cattle, tools, wagons—and receive back what they needed for their support. The remaining property would be divided among the poor so that everyone could have a farm or shop. Each year, after a family had provided for itself, the surplus would again go to a common storehouse, where the poor could find aid. This economic order, called the Law of Consecration because people dedicated their property to God, was hard to practice when most converts had nothing to spare. Eventually the church pulled back from it. But this law became the basis for the practice of tithing—giving one-tenth of one's annual income to the church. Consecration remained one of the laws of Zion, the Old Testament word for the godly society the Saints were directed to organize, thus making Mormonism both a social movement and a church.

In June 1831, soon after the revelation about Zion was received, a small band of Mormons led by Joseph Smith headed west, preaching as they went. In mid July they reached Independence, Missouri, a village on the western boundary of white settlement near present-day Kansas City. The Lord revealed to Smith that "Independence is the center place" and a temple was to be built near the courthouse. They were to purchase surrounding land and gather their families to dwell under the Law of Consecration. In early August the group dedicated the land and laid the cornerstone for a temple. Joseph Smith wrote in his history that "it was a season of joy to those present, and afforded a glimpse of the future, which time will yet unfold to the satisfaction of the faithful." He foresaw the growth of Zion with New Jerusalem as its capital.

The settlements around Independence attracted Mormon converts from all over the country. From this time on, Mormons gathered as they grew, rather than spreading out. The prevailing pattern with most other

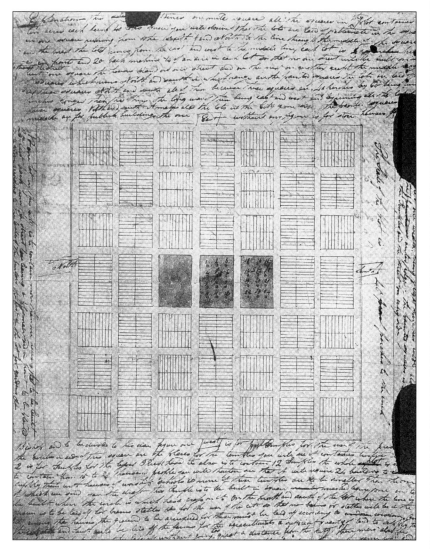

Joseph Smith's 1833 plan for laying out the site of Independence, Missouri, with temples at the center. Each town that was established by the Saints used a variation of this plan.

churches was to organize congregations and build meetinghouses wherever their members lived. Mormon missionaries instead encouraged converts to sell their farms, pack up their families, and make a long journey to a place where other members were living. Independence was the first of a number of gathering places of the Saints. The principle of gathering persisted. At various times the saints gathered in Kirtland, Ohio; Far West, Missouri; Nauvoo, Illinois; and Salt Lake City, Utah, drawing in people from all over the world to the central site, wherever it happened to

The early editions of the *Doctrine and Covenants* contained revelations to Joseph Smith. *The Pearl of Great Price* collected other of his writings, some of which claimed to be revelations to Moses and Abraham.

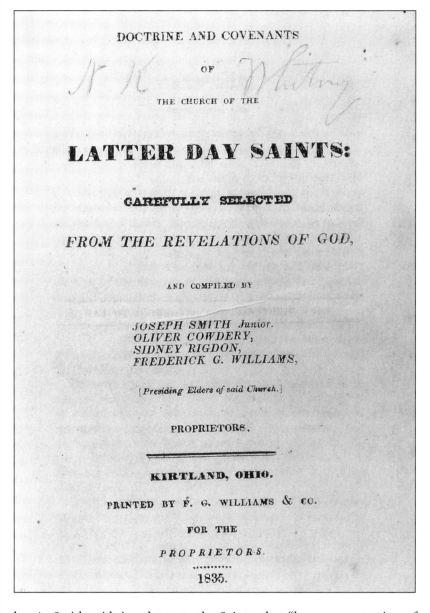

DOCTRINE AND COVENANTS

OF

THE CHURCH OF THE

LATTER DAY SAINTS:

CAREFULLY SELECTED

FROM THE REVELATIONS OF GOD,

AND COMPILED BY

JOSEPH SMITH Junior.
OLIVER COWDERY,
SIDNEY RIGDON,
FREDERICK G. WILLIAMS,

[*Presiding Elders of said Church.*]

PROPRIETORS.

KIRTLAND, OHIO.

PRINTED BY F. G. WILLIAMS & CO.

FOR THE

PROPRIETORS.
....
1835.

be. As Smith said, in a letter to the Saints, that "by a concentration of action, and a unity of effort, we can only accomplish the great work of the last days which we could not do in our remote and scattered condition."

Converts came at first by the hundreds and later by the thousands. Like other Christians, Mormons foresaw catastrophes preceding Christ's return, when war, disease, storms, and plagues would destroy the wicked as prophesied in the Bible. After warning their hearers, the Mormon missionaries offered hope that one place would be safe during the calamities. New Jerusalem, according to the revelation, would be "a land of peace, a city of refuge, a place of safety for the Saints of the Most High God; and the glory of the Lord shall be there, and the terror of the Lord also shall be there, . . . the wicked will not come unto it, and it shall be called Zion. . . . every man that will not take his sword against his neighbor must needs flee unto Zion for safety." Just a year after the dedication of the land, 830 Saints had collected around Independence. The Mormon newspaper found that it had to caution converts to slow down their coming until the church could better cope with them.

For reasons unknown, Joseph Smith himself did not remain in Independence to build up the New Jerusalem. He continued to live in Kirtland, Ohio, his headquarters and a secondary gathering place for converts. Over the next five years there, he received revelations that laid the foundation of Mormon doctrine and worship, collecting these revelations in a book called The Doctrine and Covenants.

The revelations came to Smith in many ways. Most came through the inspiration of the Holy Spirit, with Smith dictating the thoughts as they came to him. Others were visions or visitations, like the original coming of Moroni. A follower who once observed Smith receiving a revelation said that "each sentence was uttered slowly and very distinctly, and with a pause between each, sufficiently long for it to be recorded, by an ordinary writer, in longhand. . . . There was never any hesitation, reviewing, or reading back, in order to keep the run of the subject."

Two direct visitations came before moving to Kirtland, while Smith was still in New York. He said that John the Baptist appeared in May 1829, and some time later Peter, James, and John, the disciples of Jesus in the New Testament, also made visitations. Oliver Cowdery, the scribe who had written the Book of Mormon while Joseph dictated it, witnessed both visitations. Smith and Cowdery explained that the visitations were to restore the priesthood, establishing their authority to act in God's name. Protestant religions generally explained their authority to administer sacraments such as the Lord's supper or baptism by reference to the Roman Catholics, who traced their authority back to the apostle Peter. But did the Protestant reformers still have authority to act for God after their break from Catholicism? Churchmen of the period debated just who could claim to minister for Christ.

The visitations of John the Baptist and Peter, James, and John ignored the authority controversy between Protestants and Catholics by returning the Mormons to their New Testament origins. Joseph Smith claimed to receive his authority directly from a biblical source rather than relying on a linear descent of this authority through history. He called his authority the priesthood, following biblical terminology. And he claimed that it was John the Baptist, who had baptized Christ, who gave Joseph Smith and Oliver Cowdery "the Priesthood of Aaron," the Old Testament priesthood going back to Aaron, the brother of Moses. Peter, James, and John thus directly ordained Smith and Cowdery to be apostles in the Melchizedek, or higher priesthood. Mormons prize this restoration of the priesthood's authority for they believe only the authorized holders of the priesthood can perform divine ordinances or sacraments such as baptism. When a person joins the Latter-day Saints Church, he or she must be baptized by someone holding this restored authority, even if previously baptized in another church.

Smith bestowed the priesthood on virtually all male church members (though not women) and called upon them to preach and take leadership roles. Although Smith himself held the dominant position in the church, priesthood authority was otherwise widely diffused. In time he divided the priesthood's members into various groups called quorums, some invested with greater authority than others. At the head of the church stood a First Presidency of three individuals: Joseph Smith as president and two counselors. Just below the presidency were Twelve Apostles, modeled after Jesus' twelve disciples with the responsibility to carry the gospel throughout the world.

Another revelation, received in 1832, opened a view into heaven explaining how God rewarded people for their lives on earth. This vision again came to two men, Joseph Smith and Sidney Rigdon this time, the educated preacher converted in Kirtland, Ohio. While reading in the Gospel of John, Smith wondered if heaven "must include more kingdoms than one," since the scriptures say that God rewards people according to their very different deeds done on earth. The answer, Smith and Rigdon said, came in a lengthy revelation when "by the power of the Spirit our eyes were opened and our understandings were enlightened, so as to see and understand the things of God." They testified that they saw Jesus and the Father:

> And now, after the many testimonies which have been given of him, this is the testimony, last of all, which we give of him: That he lives! For we saw him, even on the right hand of God; and we heard the voice bearing record that he is the Only Begotten of the Father.

Smith and Rigdon learned of three kingdoms existing in heaven. Those who believed in Christ and lived according to the commandments went to the highest or "celestial" kingdom. People of good will who did not accept the gospel went to the "terrestrial" kingdom. And the wicked—liars, adulterers, whoremongers—headed to the third kingdom, the "telestial."

According to this vision, even wicked persons had a place in heaven, although in a lower degree of glory. For Mormons the wicked do not end up in hell, where most Christian theologies locate them, but in the third kingdom of heaven. Only those who denied the Holy Spirit after knowing it intimately and chose to give themselves to Lucifer rather than Christ went to the true hell, a dark place where Satan presided. Less wicked people could repent rather than suffering in hell forever. This vision of the "three degrees of glory," as Mormons call them, made God seem more forgiving than the traditional Christian God.

Among the visions of heaven and the future were interspersed more practical revelations like the "Word of Wisdom" that admonished followers to stay away from tobacco, alcohol, tea, and coffee and to eat fruits, vegetables, grain, and little meat, promising health, wisdom "and great treasures of knowledge, even hidden treasures." Another revelation told members to study and learn: "Seek ye out of the best books, words of wisdom; seek learning, even by study and also by faith."

In 1833, the flow of revelations was interrupted by the first of many attacks on the Mormon community. Mormon beliefs and the practice of gathering their followers set off violent opposition, and the little gathering of Saints around Independence was the first to suffer. In August 1833, Oliver Cowdery arrived in Kirtland with the disturbing news that the Missouri Saints had been told to leave the county. All through the summer, hoodlums had ridden into Mormon settlements, breaking windows, shooting into houses, and burning haystacks. In July a manifesto with hundreds of signatures attacked the Mormons and declared that they must leave immediately, or the other citizens would "use such means as may be sufficient to remove them." A mass meeting on July 20 turned into a mob of several hundred men who dumped the Mormon press with its paper and type into the street. They pulled Edward Partridge, the ranking church leader, out of his house and demanded that he tell all the Mormons to leave immediately. When he protested, they threw him to the ground, kicked him, stripped him, smeared his naked body with tar and acid, and covered him with feathers. The lieutenant-governor of the state witnessed this abuse but did not stop it. Under such pressure and with no protection from the government, the Mormons agreed to leave, half by the following January and the rest in the spring.

The pressure against the Mormons around Independence had been building for over a year as their numbers increased, multiplying the sources of irritation. The old settlers disliked competition from Mormon stores and tradesmen, as well as the bidding up of land prices that came with new population pressures. And the mostly Yankee Mormons did not sympathize with slavery. Missouri's primarily southern old settlers feared that the few free black converts who were joining the Saints in Independence would corrupt the settlers' slaves. Above all, however, it was the Mormon religion itself that repulsed the old settlers. They feared that only the dregs of society would be attracted to such beliefs. As the settlers said in their manifesto, these "deluded fanatics" claimed to "hold

personal communication and converse face to face with the Most High God; to heal the sick by laying on hands; and, in short, to perform all the wonder-working miracles wrought by the inspired Apostles and Prophets of old."

These strange Mormons also threatened the old settlers by openly declaring that God had given them the land. That may have seemed far-fetched, but as the Mormon population grew, the old settlers faced a real danger. By 1833 the Mormons comprised nearly a third of the population of Jackson County, in which Independence was located. When they achieved a majority, as they apparently soon would, they could elect county officials and control the local government. From being a few mis-guided neighbors, the Mormons had become a major political force. The

Cultural and religious dif-ferences, as well as the feared loss of political control, led to the violent expulsion of the Saints from Jackson County, Missouri, in 1833. Homes and barns were demol-ished, crops destroyed, and families driven away.

Kirtland Temple, visible on a hill in this early photograph, was completed and dedicated in 1836. One eyewitness claimed that a shaft of light shone on the steeple at the dedication.

fear of Mormon political domination was the common factor in the various persecutions from this time on.

In October the Missourians heard that the Mormons might decide, despite the persecutions, to stay on their lands. They had hired a law firm and were preparing to do battle in court. The irate settlers immediately attacked. In late October they broke down the doors of Mormon cabins, tore off their roofs, and stoned and beat the men. Screaming women and children fled into the woods. When the Mormons tried to defend themselves, a company of settlers claiming to be militia confiscated their arms. As news spread that the Mormons were unarmed, the mob struck again, wrecking, burning, or pillaging 200 cabins and forcing 1,200 people out into a rising November gale. The Saints gathered in the cold rain on the bank of the Missouri River and escaped to the other side.

This Missouri violence stunned Joseph Smith. "Oh, my God, what shall I do in such a trial as this," his mother heard him say. The revelations he had received had designated Independence as the central gathering place, but now the Saints had been driven from their promised land. The Kirtland, Ohio, Saints tried to assist their brothers and sisters, but the Missouri state government was uncooperative and the old settlers remained hostile. The Missouri Saints therefore had to find new land or wait for a chance to return. Temporarily, they found refuge across the river in Clay County.

Frustrated and angered by the sufferings of the Missouri Saints, Joseph Smith began to develop Kirtland as a second gathering place. A temple had already been planned there in addition to the one in Independence, and work began on it in 1833. The idea for a temple was broached when the Mormons outgrew their first log meetinghouse and required larger quarters. The other denominations in town had been satisfied to put up small churches a few years after starting out, but Smith was not interested in small church buildings. He decreed that the Mormons would construct a huge structure for this remote village: a building 55 feet in width and 65 feet long, with two floors—one for worship and the other for a school.

The construction of such a large building required a great effort from the small band of Mormons. Men labored on the building while trying to support their families. Members sacrificed to purchase materials and pay the full-time workers. While the

Parley P. Pratt's *Voice of Warning and Instruction* was among the first books published by the Latter-day Saints. It was widely used by missionaries proclaiming the message of the gospel.

A

VOICE OF WARNING

AND

INSTRUCTION TO ALL PEOPLE,

CONTAINING

A DECLARATION OF THE FAITH AND DOCTRINE OF THE CHURCH OF THE LATTER DAY SAINTS,

COMMONLY CALLED MORMONS.

BY P. P. PRATT, MINISTER OF THE GOSPEL.

Behold the former things are come to pass, and new things do I declare : before they spring forth, I tell you of them.—Isa. xlii. 9.

Produce your cause, saith the LORD ; bring forth your strong reasons, saith the King of Jacob.—Isa. xli. 21

New=York:

PRINTED BY W. SANDFORD, 29 ANN-ST.

MDCCCXXXVII.

1837

Mormons worked on the building, they prepared spiritually for an "endowment of power" that was to come when the temple was completed. Those words, repeated a number of times in the revelations, suggested an outpouring of the Spirit similar to the Day of Pentecost in the New Testament, when Peter and the original apostles received supernatural spiritual gifts. To prepare themselves, the men met in the unfinished building to study and pray. On one occasion Joseph Smith washed their feet, as Jesus had done for his disciples. Some people reported visions, and in the dedication week in late March 1836 many saw a great light hovering around the temple and heard a rushing wind as on the Day of Pentecost; others glimpsed angels. Joseph Smith and Oliver Cowdery said they saw the Lord, whose face "shone above the brightness of the sun; and his voice was as the sound of rushing waters, even the voice of Jehovah." They believed He had come to accept the temple.

Once the temple was completed, the Saints suffered a letdown. The local economy had been built on borrowed money, and when work on the temple ceased, an important source of funds dried up. In 1837, to bolster the economy, Joseph Smith tried to organize a bank that could lend funds to establish local industry. The state denied him a charter, but

This ten-dollar note issued by the Kirtland Safety Society in March 1837 is signed by Joseph Smith, Jr., and Sidney Rigdon. Three months later, Joseph Smith disassociated himself from the private financial institution, which failed to gain public confidence and closed later that year.

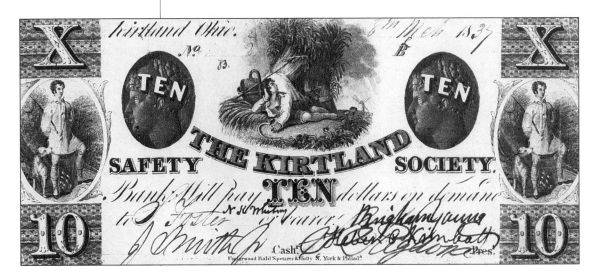

he went ahead with a joint stock company that issued paper money for local use. The whole United States was at that time on the brink of a severe depression, so the money had little value. Smith hoped to use the bank's money to build up the Kirtland economy, but these plans were doomed.

When the local economy collapsed, in the midst of a nationwide depression, Joseph Smith was held responsible, even by some of his own followers. Many of the Mormon leaders repudiated his leadership and left the church. In the fall of 1837, he and his family fled to the area in Missouri where the Independence Saints had found a home. Soon afterward, most of the Kirtland Saints, abandoning the temple on which they had so long labored, followed him to Missouri. When Smith arrived there in March 1838, the church had suffered persecution and defections within its own ranks and had many enemies and few friends. But it was far from collapse. By 1838 the church's mission was well defined, and thousands of Mormons remained loyal to their prophet, believing he was leading them in the work of God.

Chapter 3

Nauvoo, 1838–46

ow long can rolling waters remain impure? What power shall stay the heavens? As well might man stretch forth his puny arm to stop the Missouri river in its decreed course, or to turn it up stream, as to hinder the Almighty from pouring down knowledge from heaven upon the heads of the Latter-day Saints.

—Doctrine and Covenants, 121:33

The setbacks that Joseph Smith suffered before his move to Missouri in 1838 would likely have broken a less resilient man. But the expulsion of the Saints from Independence, the defection of his closest followers in Kirtland, and his personal sorrow when twins born to Emma died at birth—none of these blunted his resolve. At Far West, in Missouri, he laid plans for yet another Mormon city, selected a site for a temple, and called the Saints to gather at still another place of refuge.

But Joseph Smith and the Mormon church were to pass through even more trials. Within a year of his arrival there, his plans for Far West lay in ruins. Smith himself was in jail and the Missouri mob, supported by the government, was driving the Mormons from the state. The breakdown of the truce occurred quickly, once again in a contest for political control. Initially, the Missouri government organized a region for the Mormons in the north-central part of the state, on the theory that they should have a space of their own in which to live in peace. However, the boundary

Nauvoo was a Mississippi River boom town about the same size as Chicago in the mid-1840s. Its prosperity depended, however, on the influx of Mormon converts. When the Saints left, the town declined rapidly and soon turned into a sleepy village.

Lilburn Boggs, governor of Missouri, witnessed the Mormons' expulsion from Jackson County and later issued the order to drive them from the state. A Mormon was accused of trying to assassinate the governor.

between the Mormons and other settlers could not be maintained. Non-Mormon settlers moved into the Mormon counties, Caldwell and Daviess, and conflict broke out. The predictable explosion occurred at an August election in 1838. There the non-Mormon settlers tried to block the Mormons from casting their ballots and a fight started when the Mormons refused to back down.

This time the Mormons resolved to defend themselves. Joseph Smith himself rode with a group of fellow Mormons to the scene of the election fight as soon as he heard the news, though by then the settlers had dispersed. The Mormons had been galvanized to action by a Fourth of July oration in which Sidney Rigdon had declared, "We will never be the aggressors, we will infringe on the rights of no people; but shall stand for our own until the death. . . . No man shall be at liberty to come into our streets, to threaten us with mobs, for if he does, he shall atone for it before he leaves the place." These warning words ignited the already contentious atmosphere. Even before the election fight, unofficial bands of Mormons harassed anyone unfriendly to the Saints.

As conflicts mounted, Missourians burned Mormon cabins and haystacks. When a Mormon militia unit engaged Missouri troops, deaths occurred on both sides. Highly exaggerated reports of this encounter reached Missouri governor Lilburn Boggs, an old enemy from Independence, who issued an order to all citizens to drive the Mormons from the state. And if the citizens could not expel the Mormons, they should exterminate them. Emboldened by this order, a mob of two hundred men deputized as militia descended on the small Mormon settlement Haun's Mill and murdered everyone in sight, including a seventy-year-old man and a ten-year-old boy.

The Mormons tried to defend themselves but were hopelessly outnumbered. The militia moved into the Mormon settlement at Far West and there captured Joseph Smith, charged him with treason before an illegally convened court-martial, and sentenced him to death by firing squad. A courageous militia officer refused to carry out this sentence of drumhead justice, and instead Smith was sent off to jail and the Mormons were ordered to leave the state. While Smith languished in prison in Liberty, Missouri, the Saints, driven once more from their homes and farms in winter, trudged eastward across the state, directed by Brigham Young, the senior member of the Quorum of the Twelve Apostles, the leading council of the church.

The citizens of Illinois across the Mississippi from Missouri received the Mormon refugees sympathetically when they arrived in early 1839. Outsiders could see that the Mormons had been persecuted for their religious beliefs and took their side against the Missourians. But the good feeling was not to last: five years later, an Illinois mob was to murder Smith and, two years after that, force the Mormons to leave—once again in midwinter. In Illinois as in Missouri, the Mormons tested their non-Mormon fellow Americans' sympathy to the breaking point. People who tolerated most other religions considered the Mormons a threat to society and forced them out. Like Catholics and abolitionists in other states who also suffered at the hands of mobs in this period, Mormons fell outside the limits of American tolerance.

In 1839, however, people on both the Illinois and Iowa sides of the Mississippi welcomed the new settlers. New immigrants meant more business for shopkeepers and artisans, and more land sales for speculators. Local politicians, seeing the Mormons as prospective voters, offered hospitality. Joseph Smith made the most of this welcoming attitude when he joined the main body of the Mormon church in the spring of 1839. While he was being moved from one jail to another in Missouri, the guard let it be known to him that he should escape, having become an embarrassment to the government. Feeling no obligation to Missouri, Smith and his companions crossed safely to Illinois. On the banks of the Mississippi, he made plans for another city which he called Nauvoo, a Hebrew word meaning "the city beautiful."

At a time when the church had few financial resources, suffered from internal division, and was struggling to begin again, Joseph Smith made

An interior view of Joseph and Emma Smith's first Nauvoo home (called the Homestead), shows a modest but practical interior. The earliest Saints' homes were often small, primitive, wood frame or log buildings, but they were preferable to the tent and wagon shelters many lived in until their new homes could be built.

one of his boldest moves. Instead of gathering his strongest leaders around him to help build the new city, he assigned many of them to carry the Mormon message to Great Britain. A vanguard group had blazed the way in 1837, and in 1839 eight of the Twelve Apostles left to join them. Under the leadership of the senior member, Brigham Young, those missionaries converted thousands of new members. Turmoil in British religion and disruptions caused by the industrial revolution had left many in England searching for a religious anchor, and Mormonism offered something solid. In 1840 the convert immigrants began to arrive in Nauvoo, strengthening the church and making that city nearly as large as Chicago by 1846.

Joseph Smith's plans for Nauvoo proved to be more ambitious than ever. He purchased—on credit—large tracts of land on both sides of the Mississippi River and resold them to the Saints as they arrived in Nauvoo. Because the flats where the city was to rise were marshy from water seepage, drainage ditches had to be dug. To develop the city's commercial potential, a canal was planned through the center of town and a dam was designed to harness the power of the Mississippi. Foreseeing an increase in visitors as the city grew in wealth and fame, Joseph Smith started work on a large hotel at the water's edge to accommodate guests inquiring about Mormonism.

Smith wanted the civil government to be in Mormon hands to protect the Saints from persecution while the city grew, because in Missouri both the county and the state governments had turned against them. Hoping for help from the federal government, Joseph Smith went to the federal government in Washington in the summer of 1839 to seek redress. But President Martin Van Buren felt bound by the principle of states' rights not to interfere. Thus, with no assurance of protection from the state or federal governments, the Mormons felt they needed to control the local government themselves if there were to be any hope for peace.

Some Mormon poineer children had beautiful toys like this period doll brought to Nauvoo by a young child . The head was made of porcelain and the hairstyle reflects the style of the 1840s.

The Nauvoo city charter, obtained from the Illinois legislature in December 1840, provided the desired safeguards. It established city courts where assailants could be tried before judges elected by Nauvoo residents and juries chosen from the Mormon population. No longer could a mob attack the Saints with impunity. For added protection, the charter authorized the city to organize a Nauvoo legion, or militia, of five thousand men. Joseph Smith was chosen as both mayor and lieutenant-general of the militia, a combination of church and state power that offended Illinois residents.

Within the little kingdom formed by the city charter, Joseph Smith instructed the Saints from the revelations that came to him. Added rituals gave new purposes for the temple that was soon announced. At Kirtland the temple had been a place for worship and instruction, a general assembly building serving many groups. Now the Nauvoo revelations designated special rituals for members alone, to be observed only in the temple. From a public meeting space, the temple

The Mormon Temple at Nauvoo, completed in December 1845, contained meeting and school rooms, plus special rooms for temple ordinances such as baptism for the dead. Mormons worked on the temple up to the last minute before their expulsion from Nauvoo so that people could participate in the temple ordinances. Thomas M. Easterly took this daguerreotype of the completed temple in 1850.

became a site for religious sacraments. When completed, the Nauvoo temple had general meeting rooms on the first two floors, like the Kirtland temple, but its basement and top floor were reserved for sacred rituals. One of these was baptism for the dead. Smith taught that those who had passed on without being baptized could receive the sacrament posthumously, so that all of humanity could eventually receive the Christian gospel.

One of Joseph Smith's most controversial revelations involved another temple ritual. In a revelation on marriage and family life, he was told that a husband and wife could be "sealed" together for eternity in the temple, and their children would then be theirs forever. In addition, the revelation specified that a man could be sealed to more than one wife. The binding of man and wife for eternity was not shocking, and in fact accorded with the beliefs of other Christians that families continued after death. The hard part was the revelation about multiple wives, which was in fact a return to the practice of the Old Testament patriarchs. Polygamy, as it was commonly called, or plural marriage, as the Mormons referred to it, ran head-on against the most basic moral principles of the time.

Foreseeing difficulties with plural marriage, Smith was slow to teach the doctrine. He may have received the revelation as early as 1831 and have made tentative efforts to comply with the principle then. But the opposition of his wife Emma stopped him from saying more. At last, in Nauvoo in 1843 he explained the doctrine to others. With great reluctance, many husbands and wives complied, after receiving spiritual confirmation of the

A Nauvoo membership certificate signed by Joseph Smith for Sister Martha Goforth. The certificates assured acceptance in Latter-day Saint congregations as people moved from place to place.

> To whom it may concern:
> This certifies that I baptised Martha Goforth on sunday the 7th day of April, 1844, and confirmed her by the laying on of my hands for the gift of the Holy Ghost, as a member of the Church of Jesus Christ of Latter Day Saints.
> Given under my hand at the city of Nauvoo this 9th day of April 1844.
>
> Joseph Smith
> President of the Church of
> Jesus Christ of Latter Day Saints,

doctrine's validity. Smith knew that publicizing plural marriage would bring the wrath of society down on the Saints. But news of the practice could not be contained. Rumors of plural marriage were whispered about, fueling internal opposition to Joseph Smith in the final year of his life.

Eternal marriage and the other temple ordinances were not the only doctrines to carry Mormonism beyond the bounds of conventional Christian belief. In April 1844, two and a half months before he was to die, Joseph Smith delivered his most radical sermon. In it he made two startling pronouncements. The first was that individual people were as eternal as God; human intelligence had not been created but had instead existed forever. The second was that people could, by faithful compliance with God's commandments, become like Him, in fact become gods themselves. Joseph argued that God was not a totally different order of being from humans. Rather, He had once passed through mortal experience and was now teaching His children to be gods just as parents teach their children to become adults. "The plan of salvation," as Mormons call it, is the progression of the spirit from its existence before earthly life through its mortal existence, where the spirit obtains a body, to resurrection, when spirit and body are eternally joined, to continue forever in one of the three degrees of glory. In the celestial degree, the highest, those who listened to the Holy Spirit, had faith in Christ, and lived valiantly while on earth might become like God. This history of the individual spirit is the Mormon explanation of life's deepest meaning.

While Joseph Smith was teaching these extraordinary new doctrines, opposition from many sides was hampering his efforts. The Missouri government came to regret allowing him to escape in 1839 and now planned to try him for resisting the Missouri militia. And he was also considered an accomplice in an attempt on the life of Lilburn Boggs, the governor who had issued the Mormon extermination order. Officers with papers to serve on Smith came to Illinois, forcing him into hiding during much of 1842 and 1843.

While the Missourians were stalking Smith, Whig politicians in Illinois and their supporting newspapers had turned on the Mormons.

Their switch from the Whig to the Democratic party upon receiving support from a Democrat sparked the enmity. Thomas Sharp, a Whig politician and editor of the *Warsaw Signal*, a paper published a few miles downriver from Nauvoo, initiated a bitter campaign to discredit the Mormons. Sharp wrote that "under the sacred garb of Christianity" they "perpetrate the most lawless and diabolical deeds that have ever, in any age of the world, disgraced the human species." He accused the Mormons of counterfeiting, theft, and sexual immorality. He called Joseph Smith a religious tyrant who held his people in complete subjection by "the knavish pretension that he receives fresh from heaven divine instructions." Sharp convinced some citizens that Smith should be assassinated.

It was in the end Joseph Smith himself who provided the ammunition needed to bring about his murder. In June 1844, the Nauvoo city council ordered a dissenting newspaper closed down. The dissenters thought that Joseph Smith, as both mayor and lieutenant-general of the militia, had too much power. They opposed what they considered his delusions of grandeur about constructing a kingdom to rule the world and his teaching of polygamy that ran contrary to established morality. The dissenters, some of them high-ranking church officials, wanted to hold on to earlier Mormon doctrines but reject Smith's most recent teachings. The *Nauvoo Expositor* rallied support for a reformed Mormon church. This newspaper had published just one issue when the city acted. Smith and the city council, concerned at the enmity toward Mormons in the surrounding county and knowing that outraged Nauvoo Mormons were threatening to close the press themselves, took action. Mayor Smith, with the council's backing, ordered the city marshal to destroy the press, scatter the type, and burn any available papers. Other presses had been shuttered on similar grounds in other places, and technically the mayor had a legal right to close down a public nuisance (though not to destroy the press). But the action was a public relations disaster, proof positive to the *Warsaw Signal* that Joseph Smith had to be stopped: "Citizens arise, one and all!!! Can you stand by, and suffer such infernal devils! to rob men of their property

The Articles of Faith

Joseph Smith wrote out the following 13 principles in 1842. Though not a formal creed or an exhaustive summary, this list includes the church's basic beliefs.

1. We believe in God the Eternal Father, and in his son Jesus Christ, and in the Holy Ghost.

2. We believe that men will be punished for their own sins and not for Adam's transgression.

3. We believe that through the atonement of Christ all mankind may be saved by obedience to the laws and ordinances of the Gospel.

4. We believe that the first principles and ordinances of the Gospel are: first, Faith in the Lord Jesus Christ; second, Repentance; third, Baptism by immersion for the remission of sins; fourth, Laying on of hands for the gift of the Holy Ghost.

5. We believe that a man must be called of God, by prophecy, and by the laying on of hands by those who are in authority, to preach the gospel and administer in the ordinances thereof.

6. We believe in the same organization that existed in the Primitive Church, namely, apostles, prophets, pastors, teachers, evangelists, and so forth.

7. We believe in the gift of tongues, prophecy, revelation, visions, healing, interpretation of tongues, and so forth.

8. We believe the Bible to be the word of God as far as it is translated correctly; we also believe the Book of Mormon to be the word of God.

9. We believe all that God has revealed, all that He does now reveal, and we believe that He will yet reveal many great and important things pertaining to the Kingdom of God.

10. We believe in the literal gathering of Israel and in the restoration of the Ten Tribes; that Zion (the New Jerusalem) will be built upon the American continent; that Christ will reign personally upon the earth; and, that the earth will be renewed and receive its paradasaical glory.

11. We claim the privilege of worshiping Almighty God according to the dictates of our own conscience, and allow all men the same privilege, let them worship how, where, or what they may.

12. We believe in being subject to kings, presidents, rulers, and magistrates, in obeying, honoring, and sustaining the law.

13. We believe in being honest, true, chaste, benevolent, virtuous, and in doing good to all men; indeed, we may say that we follow the admonition of Paul—We believe all things, we hope all things, we have endured many things, and hope to be able to endure all things.

   If there is anything virtuous, lovely, or of good report, or praiseworthy, we seek after these things.

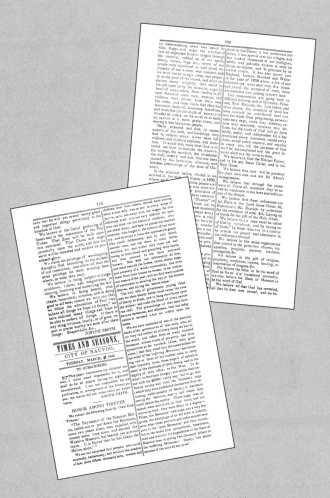

The Articles of Faith were written by Joseph Smith to sum up Mormon beliefs for an inquiring Chicago newspaperman. They are the closest the church ever came to composing a creed.

Mormons also believe in written scripture. They believe in the Bible and in the ethical and spiritual teachings of Jesus Christ. They believe that their church is a latter-day restoration of the fullness of Christ's teachings, with full authority, ordinances, and an understanding of the Godhead and the plan of salvation. Mormons consider themselves Christians who believe in continued revelation from God. Mormons believe that the current President of the Church, as Prophet, Seer, and Revelator, holds the necessary keys to communicate with Deity.

VOL. II.—NO. 27. NEW-YORK, SATURDAY, AUGUST 23, 1856. PRICE FIVE CENTS.

Latter-day Saints have a long and extensive publication history. This bold masthead from *The Mormon*, published weekly from 1855 to 1857, expresses many LDS sentiments about freedom of the press, including "Mormon creed, Mind your own business," and "U.S. Constitution Given by the Inspiration of God."

rights, without avenging them. We have no time for comment! Everyman will make his own. Let it be with powder and ball!"

When writs for his arrest were issued from the nearby county seat, Joseph Smith hesitated. He feared for his life in the hands of the county officers, having had experience with local government before, and Sharp was now telling his readers that "you will be doing your god and your country service, in aiding us to rid earth of a most heaven-daring wretch." Accordingly, Smith started west. The Saints could follow him to a place outside the United States, he reasoned, beyond the reach of hostile mobs. With most of the continent west of the Rocky Mountains under the jurisdiction of Mexico, the Mormons could find a place where U.S. citizens would not trouble them. He crossed the Mississippi River to Iowa, but not for long. When he heard that the Saints thought he was deserting them he returned and gave himself up.

After his arrest, Joseph Smith was taken to the county seat at Carthage, a few miles from Nauvoo. There he and a few friends were imprisoned, as much for safekeeping as to keep him confined. The Illinois governor, realizing that a riot was brewing, came to Carthage and personally assured Smith of his safety. Then the governor left for Nauvoo to quiet the Saints and confiscate their arms.

On June 27, 1844, while the governor was away from Carthage, a hundred men with blackened faces crept up to the jail where Smith was detained. They broke into the prison and fired into the Mormon cell. A musketball hit Hyrum Smith, Joseph's brother, who died immediately, and another man was wounded. Joseph went to the window to make an appeal. A shot immediately struck him, and he fell out the window to the ground, then raised himself against a well and died. When a cry went up that the Mormons were coming, the mob fled.

The governor rushed back, too late, but then fled himself for fear the Mormons would ravage the county in retribution. Stunned by the loss, the Mormons did nothing, however. The bodies of Joseph and Hyrum Smith were brought back to Nauvoo. The Saints mourned the death of their prophet, unable to believe that the man who had escaped so many attempts on his life had at last fallen.

On June 27, 1844, Joseph Smith was shot in the upstairs window of a jail in Carthage, Illinois, and fell to the ground below.

"The Two Martyrs," an engraving of Hyrum (left) and Joseph Smith. John Taylor, a witness to the martyrdom, wrote, "In life they were not divided, and in death they were not separated."

News of the disaster spread rapidly to Mormon congregations throughout the country. All the missionaries, including the members of the Twelve Apostles, returned to Nauvoo to confer on how to carry on after the prophet's death. Smith had talked about the succession of leadership, but not definitively. On some occasions he spoke as if authority would pass to his son or to members of his family. On other occasions, he told the Twelve Apostles that they would succeed him. In this moment of uncertainty, senior apostle Brigham Young arrived in Nauvoo in time for a meeting to discuss the possible successors. Young proposed that the Twelve Apostles had received their authority from Smith to lead the church and it was they who should take charge, acting as a body. That same day and afterward, others made rival claims. Sidney Rigdon, long closely associated with Smith, thought he should assume the leadership. William Smith, a brother of Joseph, felt the right was his. Each of these attracted some followers, but the majority of the church accepted Brigham Young.

Brigham Young in 1850, a few years after he assumed the leadership of the church following Joseph Smith's death. Young claimed authority as the senior member of the Quorum of the Twelve Apostles.

Beyond Nauvoo, many Mormons held back their support, though, and when the majority of the Mormons later went west to Utah, these scattered Saints remained behind. In 1860 many coalesced into the Reorganized Church of Jesus Christ of Latter-day Saints and asked Joseph Smith's son, Joseph Smith III, to be their leader and prophet. Joseph's wife Emma, who stayed in Nauvoo and remarried, joined this group under her son's leadership. Although they had much in common, the two Mormon churches never came back together and in recent years have drifted still further apart.

Joseph Smith's murderers were never brought to justice. Out of some sixty suspects, nine men were indicted, but their trial yielded no convictions. The enemies of the Saints not only went unpunished but their animosity toward the Mormons remained high. Not long after the trial, a mob trying to drive Mormons from outlying settlements burned more than two hundred houses as well as barns and crops. Utter lawlessness broke out. On one occasion a mob drove a sympathetic non-Mormon sheriff out of Carthage, whereupon he deputized a Mormon posse to regain control of the town. The governor, fearing chaos, urged Brigham Young to leave. The commission that delivered the

Thirteen-year-old Mary
Ann Broomhead embroi-
dered this remembrance of
the martyrdom in Nauvoo.

message warned that if the Mormons did not leave they would be forcibly expelled, so Young agreed to go. Of course, no one would buy Mormon property, knowing it would soon fall into their hands anyway. In the end, an estimated $2 million worth of homes, buildings, and land was left behind.

In the midst of this crisis, in the fall of 1845 the Saints worked feverishly on the Nauvoo temple, determined to fulfill the commandment to complete the structure before they left. The workmen took their guns to work along with their tools and labored while guards kept watch. On December 10, 1845, the building was far enough along for religious ordinances to begin. Night and day, for the next two months more than five thousand people went through the temple rituals as the building was completed.

Then it was all abandoned. On February 5, 1846, under renewed pressure from the government, the first group of Saints crossed the Mississippi on a fleet of flatboats and skiffs to begin the long trek across Iowa. Others followed through the spring, leaving only the feeble and poor behind. Antagonized by even this pitiful remnant, a mob of seven or eight hundred men laid siege to the city with small artillery and gave the stragglers just two hours to get out. The last of the Saints fled the city on September 17, 1846, putting out fourteen thousand homeless refugees from their own country onto the road west. In November 1848, the temple the Saints had labored to complete during their last weeks in the city was burned by an arsonist.

The sixteen years since the organization of the church in 1830 had brought triumphs—thousands of converts, the construction of two temples, and the building of a city—but also many sorrows. The United States, supposedly a haven of religious and political freedom, had failed to make room for this beleaguered people. In place after place, the local citizenry had forcibly expelled the Mormons without regard for their rights or consideration of their suffering. Mormons had lost their farms and houses and even their lives. Having failed to build a Zion within the United States, the Saints now sought refuge in the West, beyond the nation's boundaries.

The exodus from Nauvoo began on February 4, 1846, earlier than planned. The Saints were forced to move in the dead of winter for fear of attack by people in the surrounding county.

Chapter 4

The Westward Trek, 1846–69

beheld the Saints coming in all directions from hills and dales, groves and prairies with their wagons, flocks and herds by the thousands. It looked like the movement of a nation.

—Wilford Woodruff, rural Iowa, 1846

By the end of Joseph Smith's life, the Mormons knew they would have to go west to find peace. They had in fact already been investigating California, Oregon, and Texas even before he was killed. When they left Nauvoo in 1846, they knew they were headed for the Rocky Mountains, though the exact destination remained uncertain.

Brigham Young, who led them on this heroic migration, was poorly prepared to direct a massive movement of people. Trained as a carpenter, his only administrative experience had been as the head of the Twelve Apostles, yet he brilliantly engineered and carried out the westward trek. In the fall of 1845, when the Nauvoo Saints were anticipating their removal, Young conducted a census of the Saints to estimate their resources. He counted 3,285 families with 2,508 wagons and 1,892 more under construction. He organized this collection of people into administrative units of tens, fifties, and hundreds, each with its own captain to regulate affairs. Young called the group the Camp of Israel. Speaking for God in the only revelation he ever wrote down,

Maneuvering wagons over the narrow, winding Mormon Trail took great skill and daring. Ruts from the wagon wheels are still visible today on parts of the Trail.

he admonished them to "go thy way and do as I have told you, and fear not thine enemies; for they shall not have power to stop my work."

No amount of organization or encouragement could have prevented suffering along the cold, rainy Iowa trail in winter. But the impatient people of Illinois forced the group to leave before they were ready. In February 1846 the first wagons rumbled down Parley Street in Nauvoo and were ferried across the Mississippi by flatboat. When the river froze a few weeks later, some crossed the ice bridge. One woman recorded that nine women gave birth to babies on that first frozen night, across the Mississippi at Montrose, Iowa. With inadequate food and no shelter, the Saints limped across three hundred miles of Iowa territory and Indian tracts to the Missouri River. The bad February weather continued as they camped, crossed swollen streams, and buried their dead. Four months later, in mid June, the first group reached the Nebraska border.

Still, they bore up bravely. William C. Clayton had left his pregnant wife Diantha in Nauvoo. When he heard that she had given birth to a healthy son, he turned an English folk song into a Mormon hymn of hope.

> Come, come, ye Saints, No toil nor labor fear;
> But with joy wend your way.
> Though hard to you this journey may appear,
> Grace shall be as your day.
> 'Tis better far for us to strive
> Our useless cares from us to drive
> Do this, and joy your hearts will swell—
> All is well! All is well!

The cooperative Mormons helped each other as they traveled west. They established permanent settlements at Garden Grove and Mt. Pisgah in Iowa, planting crops and building little houses for later migrants. Subsequent pioneers, after trudging through miles of mud, found comfort and food at these way stations. After two weeks at Garden Grove, the Saints reported that they had cleared three hundred acres of land and planted crops. Whenever they stopped, the men fanned out to work for wages or make things to sell or trade. Their brass band played concerts for cash or corn. At the Missouri River, where they finally arrived in June,

they settled in to make a base camp for the long trek to the Rockies. At what is now Council Bluffs, Iowa, they built a "Grand Encampment" stretching nine miles east from the river. We can see from diary entries that the Saints saw themselves as modern children of Israel, cast out to wander in the wilderness until they could return to their Promised Land in Jackson County, Missouri.

Meanwhile, the United States had declared war against Mexico, and to raise needed cash Brigham Young mobilized a battalion of Mormons for the Southwest campaign. The five hundred enlisted men traveled west at army expense, with their wages helping the rest of the group and at the same time demonstrating Mormon loyalty to the United States.

Although it provided income, the Mormon battalion drained the Saints of manpower at a crucial moment. A total of 490 men and 12 boys marched away, accompanied by 20 women, who cooked and washed for the troops. Many never saw their families again. The volunteers served a

Mormons cross the ice-covered Mississippi after being driven from Nauvoo. Some 20,000 people wintered at Council Bluffs in Iowa Territory before making the long trek to Utah.

The last of the Mormons were forced out of Nauvoo with few provisions. In October 1846, many quail flew into their camp and were cooked and eaten, saving the starving Mormons. The Saints saw this as a miracle paralleling a similar incident in ancient Israel.

year, marching to Fort Leavenworth, Kansas, and eventually to San Diego, California, a distance of more than two thousand miles, the longest U.S. march in military history. Some even doubled the length of their march by returning home. Newman Bulkley walked back to Nebraska, covering more than five thousand miles in all, half the time with bare feet. When he got back, he had been gone for two years and three months and was dirty and ragged, without a shirt, wearing the same old coat he had left in. Others rejoined their families in the West.

As it happened, the Mormon battalion did no fighting, but ironically it assisted in making Utah and California part of the United States. After mustering out, some of the Mormon soldiers worked in California and were present at the gold strike in Sacramento in 1848.

Without many of their men, the pioneers wintered at the Missouri River. The local Indian tribe granted permission to build a settlement called Winter Quarters in Nebraska's Indian Territory north of present-day Omaha. There the Saints built more than six hundred log cabins and sod houses, a large church and a schoolhouse, and a water-powered grist-mill. Of the five thousand pioneers who stopped at Winter Quarters, various ones died of scurvy, malnutrition, or exposure: six hundred are buried in a hilltop cemetery. Another seven thousand to ten thousand Saints wintered all over southwestern Iowa and in St. Louis. After two years, when Winter Quarters reverted to the Indians, the Mormons moved across the river and built Kanesville, once a settlement of some seven thousand Mormons. There they built wagons, harvested crops, and prepared to travel west.

The sufferings of the overland pioneers were shared by a handful of Saints who sailed around the Horn, the southern tip of South America. On the same day the Nauvoo group crossed the Mississippi, 238 Mormons began a sea voyage of twenty-four thousand miles from New York to Yerba Buena (now San Francisco). The group leased an old, worn-out 450-ton cargo vessel, the *Brooklyn* and set out. One passenger, Caroline Joyce Crocheron, according to her daughter Augusta, considered her days on that leaky immigrant ship as the darkest of her life. The passengers paid $75 for passage and provisions, with half price for each of the 100 children, which was for the time a reasonable amount for a six-month journey, considering that they would have needed ten dollars a week to live at home. The ship carried all the technology of a new community: a printing press, hundreds of books, a brass cannon, a black-smith's forge, and tools enough for eight hundred men.

When storms battered the ship, the Saints lashed the women and children to their berths, even as they confidently prayed and sang. Twelve people and two cows died at sea and two babies were born, John Atlantic Burr and Georgiana Pacific Robbins. The ship sailed into Yerba Buena about July 31. When the fog lifted, the passengers saw the Stars and Stripes flying and knew they were back in United States territory. As the first arrivals under the American flag, they doubled the local population. On its next voyage, the *Brooklyn* brought the first miners to the California gold fields.

This sailing group reached the West Coast before the overland pioneers, led by Brigham Young, left Nebraska. In the spring of 1847, the overland party's advance group of about 150 men, with three women and two children, began the trip from the Winter Quarters to Salt Lake Valley. This advance party was to choose a place to settle and plant crops. They left Elkhorn, Nebraska, on April 16 in a train with seventy-two wagons plus horses, mules, oxen, cows, dogs, and some chickens. The trip went smoothly and the group caroused into the evening, arguing and playing cards. Offended by their frivolity, Brigham Young unleashed a furious blast, recalling them to the proper spirit for building a city of God and rekindling their fervor.

The easy first half of the journey stretched across the plains to Fort Laramie, Wyoming. The mountain half from there on was much harder, with the worst stretch of trail at the end, when supplies and energy were running low. On the last thirty-six miles, from the Weber River to Salt Lake Valley, the forward party slaved with ax and shovel to make even a few miles a day while Brigham Young, delirious with "mountain fever" (back and head pain), waited behind. The advance party reached Salt Lake Valley on July 21, shouting for joy to be out of the mountains. When Brigham Young arrived on July 24 he confirmed that this was the place to settle.

As the advance party arrived, another group, ten times the size of the first—mostly women and children—was setting out. Mary Isabella Horne, later a leader of women's groups, noted some figures in her trail journal. Her record shows that 1,553 people, 2,212 oxen, 124 horses, 587 cows, 358 sheep, 716 chickens, and some pigs crossed the plains: a moving agricultural village with everything but land. Mary Isabella and her family owned three wagons, each with two yokes of oxen. The wagons held farm implements, seed grain, cooking utensils, a few dishes, clothing, a small cooking stove, and a rocking chair. They carried food enough to nourish eight people for eighteen months, through the summer and winter and the following summer, until the harvest of their still-unplanted crop.

Mrs. Horne drove one wagon, the family hired a couple to drive another, and, because her husband was busy as captain of the first fifty, the Hornes' nine-year-old son Henry drove the third. Along the way the group was frightened by a buffalo herd and harassed by Indians, who demanded a payoff to let them pass. Another time, a group of Indians fancied the Hornes' baby daughter and offered a pony for her. Rebuffed, the Indians raised the offer to four ponies. Isabella felt grateful to escape from these determined braves.

The women kept house along the trail, feeding their families, and when the wagon train met Brigham Young's party returning from Utah to the Winter Quarters they prepared a feast. The women roasted a fat steer, unpacked their dishes, and improvised a table for 1,301 diners. This was no small achievement, since heavy snow was falling. During the spirited table conversation, the Indians stole forty horses.

This is the first glimpse Mormons had of the Great Salt Lake Valley from the summit of Big Mountain. Streams from the Wasatch Mountains watered the land and made farming feasible.

The wagon train finally arrived in Salt Lake Valley on October 6, 1847, after a four-month journey. They descended the mountain in the dark, guided by the flickering light of campfires on Pioneer Square. There they pitched their tents, grateful for the end of the journey.

More than three hundred wagon trains—ten thousand wagons in all—would bring Mormons to Utah over the next twenty-two years. Missionaries continued to convert new members, most of whom gathered in Zion. In the 1850s and 1860s thousands of converts from England and Scandinavia turned away from their home cultures and set their faces toward the west, where the Mormon church assimilated and resettled them in a whole new way of life. The converts typically left home in January and February, hoping to reach Utah before the next winter's snowfall. Some companies chartered ships to cross the Atlantic, with agents managing the migration and guiding the travelers at transfer points. The English novelist Charles Dickens, observing such a departure, commented on the orderliness of the group and their "special aptitude for organization." He considered them "the pick and flower of England."

The Mormons traveled by ship to New Orleans, then seven hundred miles up the Mississippi and five hundred more up the Missouri to either Kanesville or Florence, Nebraska. Alternatively, they might go by train to Iowa City and then Omaha. Wagons left Nebraska steadily for more than twenty years for the thousand-mile overland journey to Salt Lake.

Because many poor emigrants could not afford the trip, the church established a Perpetual Emigration Fund to advance travel costs, which were to be repaid after the emigrants had settled in the West. In its thirty-seven years of operation, the fund spent well over $2 million in cash and accounted for more than $10 million worth of donated equipment and services. In theory, the repayment from the emigrants was to fund additional pioneers, but in fact many were never able to repay their loans, and in 1880 much of the indebtedness was cancelled.

As heavy immigration and rising travel costs strained the church's resources, its leaders looked for ways to economize. Most wagon train travelers walked rather than rode in the overloaded, bumpy, slow wagons, and rounding up and caring for oxen on the trail took great effort. The

This statue on Temple Square in Salt Lake City commemorates the faith and sacrifice of 2,962 pioneers who walked from Iowa and Nebraska to Utah, pushing and pulling handcarts loaded with their belongings.

idea that the travelers might be able to pull their own goods in small wagons at much lower cost led to a handcart movement. Impoverished European Saints jumped at the chance to borrow nine pounds from the fund and walk from Nebraska to Utah.

The handcarts were open wagon boxes about four feet square with two large wheels. A man or woman stepped between wooden shafts in front and, with a shaft under each arm, pulled the wagon or pushed against a crossbar in front. Each cart held a few personal possessions and four or five hundred pounds of food, clothing, bedding, and cooking utensils. The leaders estimated that fifteen miles a day would bring the walkers to Utah in seventy days initially, but with a little practice they could travel faster. The handcart movement led more than three thousand poor Saints to walk with their carts to Zion between 1856 and 1860.

The handcart system required careful timing. If bad weather held up ships at sea, the walkers arrived late at Iowa City, where they could be further delayed if their carts were not ready. The first group in 1856 did not start off until June. Three companies of eight hundred immigrants, many of them unhealthy, young, or old, set out then to walk thirteen hundred miles, from the Iowa River to Salt Lake City. Short of rations at Fort Laramie, they pushed on as fast as they could. When they finally arrived in the Valley, they had traveled faster than anything else on the road.

Two other groups that first year suffered heavy casualties. The Willie and Martin companies were not able to leave Iowa City until mid and late July. The squeaking wheels of their hastily built carts were greased with tallow to quiet them, but then sand stuck to them and ground them down. Supplies failed and the leaders had to ration food even as winter came early, with long blizzards. The snow fell steadily as the trails rose to higher altitudes. Three hundred miles from Salt Lake, the pioneers ran out of flour.

On October 4, in Salt Lake City, Brigham Young heard that fourteen hundred walkers and wagon emigrants were still on the road and hastily organized help. He called for teams, teamsters, wagons, flour, and clothing. Diarist Lucy Meserve Smith noted that "the sisters stripped off their petticoats, stockings, and everything they could spare, right there in the Tabernacle [meetinghouse], and piled them into the wagons to send to the Saints in the mountains." The first rescuers were soon traveling through a snowstorm. Even after they reached the groups with their relief wagons, food, and clothing, the weary travelers still had far to go. Many had frozen fingers and toes, hands and feet and had them amputated under the most primitive conditions. This disaster underscores the monumental problems of bringing many people vast distances under difficult circumstances, as well as illustrates the tremendous will of the Mormon people to work together to benefit all.

A trail marker signed by Brigham Young reads: "Pioneers camped here June 3, 1857, making 15 miles today, all well."

In the 1860s, Mormon leaders established a transportation system whereby wagons, oxen, and teamsters loaned by Utah towns traveled east, dropping off flour supplies at settlements along the Mormon trail, then picked up immigrants at the Missouri River and hauled them west. Such trains moved more than twenty thousand people to Utah in the 1860s.

This pioneer period, from 1846 to 1869, officially ended with the completion of the transcontinental railroad. After that, converts could travel from Liverpool, England, to Ogden, Utah, in just twenty-four days instead of the old three- to five-month trip. The converted Mormons arrived in great numbers. Few came from Catholic countries, but the volume from England and Scandinavia remained high, and more and more came from Germany. More than 85,000 Mormon immigrants, and thousands of their children (whose numbers went unrecorded), came to Utah before 1887. Many later looked back and thought the trek had been the best time of their lives. The Mormon converts had been the most systematic, organized, and disciplined pioneers on the road. As the historian H. H. Bancroft describes it, it was a "migration without parallel in the world's history."

Chapter 5

Building the Kingdom, 1847–69

can very well remember with what joy and pleasure each one of our company, and even I, myself, looked upon the little growing city in the wilderness. We felt that all of our troubles and trials were practically at an end, when, as a matter of fact they had only begun.

—*Charles W. Nibley*

Left to their own preferences, the thousands of Mormon migrants who trekked to Utah would never have chosen that barren and treeless region as their home, with its salty lake, sagebrush, crickets, lizards, and rattlesnakes. Harriet Decker Young, one of Brigham's wives, recorded that on her arrival "my feelings were such as I cannot describe; everything looked gloomy and I felt heart sick." At least, the Mormons thought, no one would bother them there.

The migrants began at once to turn the desert into farmland. By nightfall of their first day, they had broken three acres of ground, and several plows. The next day they dammed the creek flowing from the mountains, bringing fresh water to their fields. Brigham Young laid out Great Salt Lake City along the lines of Joseph Smith's plan for New Jerusalem, with streets eighty-eight feet wide and twenty-foot-wide sidewalks. He reserved forty central acres for a temple. Young distributed city lots and farmland to the settlers. Each block held eight one-and-a-quarter-acre plots, with the house on each to be set back twenty feet from the street allowing for a clean, pleasant front yard. This orderly city, the flagship of

Brigham Young became the dominant figure in Utah's political and church governments. He was not concerned about the separation of church and state.

an independent, self-sufficient nation that produced and manufactured everything it needed, would be governed according to God's principles. Set apart from the industrial east by isolation and poverty, the Mormons intended to rely on their own limited resources and ingenuity.

Mary Isabella Horne, who had earlier written of her trip across the plains, first lived in a tent in the pioneer fort. The Hornes later moved into a two-room log house without doors and floors. They had brought two small windows with them, but they had to improvise their furniture.

To make a corner bed, they bored holes in two walls to insert poles, which met where the one bed leg sat on the ground. Then the Hornes inserted pegs in the logs and interlaced strips of rawhide to make a spring to hold the bedding. Packing boxes became cupboards, tables, and stools. They were fortunate to have their rocker and cookstove. For light, Isabella lit a twisted rag in a little grease in a saucer. She used soot, yellow paint and a bit of skim milk to stain the window and door frames. The family carefully rationed their flour, supplementing it with sego (mariposa) lily roots and wild parsnips, which they gathered and boiled. For breakfast and supper they ate graham (whole wheat flour) gruel, thin mush without milk or sugar. They suffered from many mice that ate their food and clothing and ran across the family in their beds until they got a kitten.

In March 1848, a storm pelted the little settlement with rain, snow, and sleet for ten days. As their homes were roofed with poles, grass, and earth, a rain of muddy water continued inside until well after the storm. The women attended to their duties while holding umbrellas over their heads.

The family records show that Joseph Horne bought four small potatoes for fifty cents from a traveler from California. Out of these he raised a bushel of fine potatoes, but the family could not eat them, because they had to be saved for seed. As the vegetables came on that year—melons, pumpkins, and squash; beets, turnips, carrots, and onions—the family rejoiced. They had had no vegetables for nearly three years and thought they had never eaten anything so good.

Then, just as their hard work, ingenuity, and rationing were about to pay off, disaster struck the flourishing crops. The promising field of spring wheat with its fat heads waved in the breezes. But quite suddenly, hordes of large, loathsome black crickets appeared. Huge crowds of lumpy, wingless insects, which as the bitter joke had it looked like a cross between a spider and a buffalo, crawled down from the mountains and moved through the fields, devouring everything in their path. The horrified Mormons could only watch as their wheat disappeared. They fought these creatures with sticks, shovels, and brooms but could not stop them. The Saints were seven hundred miles from the West Coast and a thousand from supplies in the East. Without wheat they faced starvation.

At this point came what many considered a great miracle. Seagulls from the nearby Salt Lake swooped in and began to devour the crickets. They filled their stomachs with the black creatures, disgorged them in nearby ditches, and

began again. The seagulls saved some of the grain to harvest, and the stately white birds have ever since been considered special friends to the Mormons.

The Mormons held their Sabbath meetings in the open air. The men used their teams to haul poles and green boughs from the canyon and build a bowery like the one they had had in Nauvoo, to shield the group from the scorching sun. They often gathered in each others' houses on winter evenings to sing and pray.

Howard Stansbury, a U.S. government surveyor who spent a winter in the valley while mapping the area, described the Mormons' religious services as consisting of singing, prayer, and a sermon from the pulpit.

In the early years following the arrival of the Mormon pioneers in the Salt Lake Valley, infestations of crickets threatened their badly needed crops. The arrival of seagulls, who ate the crickets, saved much of the harvest. The event became known as the miracle of the gulls.

The Mormon Battalion was recruited to fight in the Mexican-American War. In their long march from Nebraska to the Pacific, the 500 men never fired a shot at the enemy. They helped bring order to unruly California after the United States took over from California.

They used no printed ritual, and as the religious and civil leadership were one, sermons dealt with secular as well as religious matters. The Mormons, Stansbury said, believed they were guided by revelation. They firmly believed in healing the sick by the laying on of hands. Many assured him that they had seen or experienced miraculous cures. "A band of music is stationed behind the choir of singers," Stansbury noted, "and not only aids in the devotional services, but regales the audience before and after the close of the exercises."

Some Mormons thought that they would be better off in California, which had been praised by members of the Mormon battalion in the Mexican War and by passengers from the *Brooklyn*. A group of them panned out gold dust worth $60,000 from 1848 to 1851. But Brigham Young strongly supported the Salt Lake Valley location, contending that farming was a better and even a more profitable life. "You can't eat gold," he told the people. Still, the Saints profited greatly from the gold rush by trading their fresh vegetables and animals to prospective gold diggers for wagons, tools, iron, provisions, and clothing. About fifteen thousand migrants a year stopped in Salt Lake on their way to the gold fields in 1849 and 1850, giving work to blacksmiths, millers, and boardinghouses.

With ambitious plans for settling colonies north and south of Salt Lake City, Young sent out parties to explore and survey the land. They settled the valleys along the Wasatch range, where mountain water could be captured for irrigation. Next they ringed those settlements with remote colonies along important transportation routes. These included Carson Valley, Nevada, built up from 1845 to 1851; San Bernardino, California, developed in 1851; Las Vegas, Nevada, and Moab, in south-eastern Utah, in 1855; Fort Supply and Fort Bridger, Wyoming, in 1853 and 1856; and Lemhi, in northern Idaho, in 1855. The area within this ring stretched for a thousand miles north to south and eight hundred miles from east to west, encompassing one sixth of the present area of the United States. The Saints had in effect established a "Mormon corridor" to the Pacific Ocean via San Bernardino.

To populate these settlements, Brigham Young called upon people to leave Salt Lake Valley and establish new towns. He read their names from the pulpit in general conference sessions, expecting them to pack up their belongings and set out. When Elizabeth Ann Claridge's father's name was called out to settle "Muddy," a primitive site in Nevada, she sobbed and cried, even though the tears were spoiling her new white dress. A calmer friend suggested that her father might choose not to go. Elizabeth replied through her tears, "I know that my father will go and that nothing could prevent him and I should not own him as a father if he would not go

Brigham Young party in Southern Nevada on a trip to the Muddy River settlements in 1871. The church sent settlers far to the north and to the south of Salt Lake City in order to lay claim to a large inland empire.

when he is called." En route to Muddy, one of the Claridges' wagons heading up a mountain came loose and plunged over a precipice, scattering their provisions and clothing over the prairie below. As Elizabeth's father watched the wagon go he told her that one day she would have much better clothes to wear. Later, as the wife of wealthy businessman Alfred McCune, she wore elegant dresses and hats.

When Joseph Horne was sent south to grow cotton in the Dixie country of southern Utah in 1858, he could stop at small towns all along the way, several of which he had pioneered. The Mormons founded some ninety-six settlements during the first ten years after their occupation of Salt Lake Valley, and at least five hundred altogether during the nineteenth century.

The Mormon leaders organized the Latter-day Saint settlements into a Mormon state called Deseret and elected their own governor, legislature, and local officers. Utah came under the jurisdiction of the United States as a result of the war with Mexico, and Congress created the Utah Territory in 1850. President Millard Fillmore appointed Brigham Young to serve as the territorial governor.

By the spring of 1849, some six thousand Mormons were living in the Great Basin, and by 1852 there were twenty thousand. About 60 percent, or almost nine thousand, Mormons of the original Nauvoo population had followed Brigham Young west by 1850, and more were waiting to come. Perhaps 40 percent of the Mormons in the valley by then were British born.

The effort to establish industry in the valley proved disappointing. The Saints invested significant sums in a pottery, a paper mill, a sugar beet refinery, a woolen cloth factory, a sorghum molasses operation, an iron refinery, a lead mine, a silk operation, and later a cotton industry. The paper and sorghum enterprises did achieve some success, but most operations, which were chronically short of equipment, capital, and skilled labor, consumed money and effort and produced little or no profit. Tithing funds, the annual 10 percent of their incomes that members devoted to the church, supported the various industries, as did the labor of indebted immigrants paying off their travel costs when they could.

A group of Paiute Indians stop before a Mormon co-op in Salt Lake City on their way to a pow-wow in 1869. Relations between Mormons and Native Americans have always been complex and sometimes strained.

Agriculture was precarious, too. In 1855 the grasshoppers, worse than the original plague of crickets, infested the farmlands. These despised insects flew, darkening the sky, whereas the crickets at least only crawled. As thick as heavy snow, grasshoppers ate everything before them. This devastation was accompanied not only by a serious drought but by the arrival of over four thousand hungry new immigrants. Near-famine followed. The church organized its members to ward off disaster, rationing food and instituting special fast offerings. Church members were urged to go without food for twenty-four hours each month and donate that which was saved to the poor. Neighbors helped each other. Once Eliza Lyman's husband set off on church business without leaving any food, she noted, "Jane James, the colored woman, let me have two pounds of flour, it being half of what she had." All suffered during this time, but through working together none starved.

The near-famine inspired a reform movement to unify the church against a threatening world. Mormon leaders urged the following of moral principles with great intensity, interpreting the crop failure of 1855 as a divine rebuke for wastefulness and laxity. Public exhortation and private soul searching brought church and state ever closer, with govern-

Brigham Young insisted that Johnston's Army camp far to the west of the city, where it would be in no position to trouble the Saints. Pictured here are members of the army's bugle corps at Camp Floyd.

ment meetings in 1856 consisting of preaching and calls for repentance. Brigham Young, reappointed as territorial governor in 1854, ran the church and the territory like a single entity, ruling as a benevolent despot.

Several eastern justices, appointed by President James Buchanan to serve with Young, objected to this close connection of church and state. Some justices went so far as to file false reports erroneously stating that U.S. court records in Salt Lake City had been burned. A disappointed contract bidder charged that "no vestige of law and order, no protection for life or property" remained in Utah. Traders accused the church of monopolizing commerce in Indian country. Incited by these unfounded charges of tyrannical local government, and having made no investigation to verify the accusations, the United States sent federal troops to invade and control the Utah Territory.

On July 18, 1857, the first of twenty-five hundred federal troops left Fort Leavenworth, Kansas, to establish and maintain law and order in the territory. Their aim was to put down the "substantial rebellion against the laws and authority of the United States." According to President Buchanan's speech to Congress that year, Utah was under the personal despotism of Brigham Young. Buchanan accordingly named Alfred Cumming of Georgia to replace Young as governor, to restore what he called "the supremacy of the Constitution and laws within its limits."

The political basis for this move was complicated. In these last few years before the Civil War, was the government using Utah to silence the rumblings of secessionism elsewhere in the country? Was John B. Floyd, the Secretary of War and a Virginian, trying to weaken the United States army, to help the South? Was President Buchanan being opportunistic in deflecting public attention from slavery, weakening the power available to the Union in case of trouble? Would his firmness in the West discourage secession in the South? Whatever its political motivation, Mormons considered Buchanan's move persecution. Once again their peculiarities—the closeness of church and state and their practice of polygamy—strained the limits of toleration. The beleaguered Mormons saw the federal troops as invaders and prepared for war.

The church, awaiting the arrival of the army under Colonel Albert Sidney Johnston, mobilized all its settlements, calling up the Nauvoo legion, the territorial militia of three thousand men. Brigham Young called home all the missionaries and all those living in the "outposts of Zion." Settlers sacrificed valuable property in Nevada and California and returned home to defend the heartland. More than two hundred men scouted the enemy's movements and protected incoming immigrants. They harassed the federal troops, stampeding army animals, setting fire to trains, burning the country before them, blocking roads, destroying river crossings, and waking troops at night. "Take no life," they were told, "but destroy their trains and stampede or drive away their animals, at every opportunity." The Mormons even burned their own Wyoming settlements, Fort Supply and Fort Bridger, rather than allowing the troops to occupy them. A federal soldier compared their advance over the scorched earth to the retreat of Napoleon's army from Russia.

At this time of fear, suspicion, and extreme feelings, as the Mormons prepared to defend themselves, a disastrous massacre occurred at Mountain Meadows, two hundred miles south of Salt Lake City. The Fancher company, a party of Missourians migrating to California, angered some local Native Americans, who accused them of poisoning their meat and water. The Mormon settlers preparing for war, refused to sell supplies to the company, whereupon the migrants, enraged, simply helped themselves. For reasons that have never been fully understood, Mormon leaders in southern Utah proceeded to order the destruction of

United States troops entering Salt Lake City in the spring of 1858 passed Brigham Young's residence (at left) on Brigham Street, later renamed South Temple Street.

the company. The Indians and the Mormon settlers therefore killed 120 people, virtually everyone in the company except for a few young children. Brigham Young heard of the attack too late to stop it. This tragic incident, the legacy of suffering in Missouri and of the grim paranoia of the time, is a dark blot on the history of the Mormons.

To the north in Salt Lake City, Brigham Young forbade armed forces to enter the territory and ordered the militia to repel any invasion. The community was turning out bullets, cannonballs, gunpowder, and even guns. Soldiers were camped on the public square in Salt Lake City, ready to defend their city. Most of them had been driven out before. Now they had nowhere else to go, and they intended to stand firm.

Unwilling to back down in the face of Mormon resistance, the government increased the number of soldiers in the invading army and replaced their destroyed supplies. Meanwhile, Brigham Young attempted to negotiate. With the help of Pennsylvanian Thomas L. Kane, a sympathetic non-Mormon with connections in Washington, an agreement was made for Governor Cumming to enter Utah peacefully without a military escort and assume the governorship. Cumming assessed the Mormons' military readiness and satisfied himself that many of the charges against the Mormons were untrue. When his report reached Washington, President Buchanan issued an amnesty proclamation.

The federal troops, waiting back on the trail, marched through Salt Lake City to camp west of town. Uneasy at their presence, Brigham Young evacuated Salt Lake and the northern settlements, sending thirty thousand citizens and their wagons south. He was ready to abandon and burn the city. A few Mormon soldiers stood ready to torch flammable materials piled at every door. The U.S. soldiers, by then numbering fifty-five hundred, made their triumphal march through silent, deserted streets and camped forty miles away. When Young was satisfied that the soldiers were truly gone, he invited his thin, ragged followers, driving their animals, back to the northern cities and villages.

Not a bullet was shot in the Utah war, which had apparently been begun as a political maneuver. Indeed, the war brought good business as the troops bought supplies from the Mormons. And when they were called back home to fight the Civil War, the troops abandoned many of their goods to the Mormons. Even as the Mormons preached and tried to practice self-sufficiency, their greatest financial benefits came as windfalls from the gold rush's forty-niners and the army.

The Mormons had attempted to keep themselves distinct from other groups, had worked to develop economic self-sufficiency, and had tried to leave the United States. They succeeded in none of these. Their efforts at self-sufficiency failed, even as their reliance on outside groups provided a fortunate prosperity. They found themselves firmly under the direction of the United States, with their efforts at isolation steadily eroded by other western settlers as well as by improved communication and transportation. Even though they built the Deseret Telegraph themselves and their own sections of the transcontinental railroad, after 1869 they would have to cope with the changes brought by that railroad and its access to the wider world. These invasions of the Mormon heartland eventually disrupted even family life and interfered with the practice of plural marriage.

Mormon Women, 1831–90

e wish the sisters, so far as their inclinations and circumstances may permit, to learn bookkeeping, telegraphy, reporting, typesetting, clerking in stores and banks, and every branch of knowledge and kind of employment suited to their sex and according with their several tastes and capacities.

> *—Brigham Young*

In the nineteenth century, easterners considered Mormon women to be pitiful and oppressed. Besides the usual difficulties of pioneer living—the isolation, the privations, and the discomforts—they lived under the rule of "that dictator" Brigham Young. Many women lived in polygamous households as second or third wives, sharing husbands and limited incomes. Women in the East, striving for rights of their own, considered Mormon women slaves and concubines, prisoners who must be liberated from their prisons.

To their amazement, visitors to Salt Lake City found Utah women strong and independent. Brigham Young encouraged them to build the community by learning useful skills. The women helped to support their households, husbands, and other wives, and took on general community projects. Fifty years before national woman suffrage was instituted, Mormon women voted in territorial elections.

Typically, Mormon women took the initiative in Nauvoo by organizing the Relief Society in 1842. Joseph Smith approved the formation of

amuel Ashton's cabin ound 1870. Most ormons outside Salt Lake ty lived in primitive wellings until late in the th century.

Chapter 6

81

First Relief Society Meeting
Nauvoo, March 17, 1842

This decorative plate depicts the organizational meeting of the Relief Society on March 17, 1842. Joseph Smith, who formally organized the 20 women present into a society, stated: "The church was never perfectly organized until the women were thus organized."

the group "under the priesthood and after the pattern of the priesthood" as the "Female Relief Society of the City of Nauvoo." Emma Smith, Joseph Smith's wife and the Society's first president, said, "We are going to do something extraordinary . . . we expect extraordinary occasions and pressing calls." Directed to "search out the poor, and suffering, and to call on the rich for aid and thus as far as possible relieve the wants of all," the women sewed, made shirts for the temple workers, and distributed food to the hungry. The group disbanded during the western movement, but in 1867 Brigham Young's wife Eliza R. Snow reestablished the Society in Utah. He urged her to "get up societies by which they could promote the home labor of their sex."

The group undertook a wide range of activities to help women sustain themselves and benefit the community as a whole. Operating from Relief Society Halls furnished with cooking and sewing equipment, the sisters stressed cooperative activities, producing brooms, baskets, straw hats, and other items, which were sometimes sold in their own cooperative general stores. The Relief Society helped Brigham Young in his campaign to stop the flow of valuable dollars eastward to buy imported goods. Young encouraged the men to swear off imported coffee, liquor, and tobacco, and the women to stifle their frivolous desires for fashionable clothes. He ridiculed eastern fashions and encouraged simplicity, telling women to give up "their follies of dress and cultivate a modest apparel." The Relief Society encouraged women and girls to make their own "neat and comely" clothing.

It might seem that these women would have preferred a plainness and simplicity, but giving up nice things was a trial for them. They yearned to be fashionable. When Brigham Young and a group of travelers stopped in the small town of Nephi, Utah, and dined with the Claridges, young Elizabeth Claridge noted how the girls flew around to make "everything nice for the stylish city folks!" Once the company was seated at dinner, the girls slipped upstairs and "tried on all the ladies' hats."

To stop fashion-conscious women from buying from the East, Young urged them to raise silkworms, a demanding practice called sericulture, so that they could produce their own silk dresses. The obedient women planted mulberry trees and raised smelly silkworms. But the worms grew fast and tended to take over whole houses unless they were killed by ants, rats, or disease, a ghastly carnage that can only be imagined. A whole family would gather mulberry leaves to feed the hordes of silkworms. The women did in fact produce many handkerchiefs, collars, and stockings. A silk spinning and weaving factory was even built before sericulture and raising silkworms were abandoned as impractical.

Mormon women at work with silk worms. They hoped to manufacture fabric locally and thus reduce the flow of much needed cash out of the territory.

The sisters of the Relief Society also stored wheat against a possible famine. They gleaned the harvested fields for overlooked kernels and sold the eggs that their chickens laid on Sundays to purchase Relief Society grain. (Eggs laid on other days of the week were reserved for family use.) In time the women amassed huge stores of wheat in Society granaries. From these supplies the sisters loaned out seed wheat to farmers and gave out wheat for bread during droughts. Sometimes they sold wheat to help build chapels. At the time of the golden jubilee of the founding of the church, in 1880, some thirty-five thousand bushels of wheat were loaned out for seed. The sisters sent supplies to San Francisco earthquake victims in 1906 and to China the next year. In 1918 they sold two hundred thousand bushels to the U.S. government to augment dwindling wartime supplies.

The Relief Society also encouraged women to study and practice midwifery. Particularly at childbirth, Mormons felt that women should be treated by other women, as a matter of modesty. Midwife Patty Sessions, who lived to be ninety-nine, attended 3,977 births and had only two difficult cases. Hannah Sorenson claimed to have delivered four thousand babies without losing a child or a mother.

Once medical training improved in the East, Mormon men and women, who had relied on the natural and folk remedies of their time, were sent there to earn degrees. Although Mormons still believed in divine healing, Brigham Young suggested that the women dedicated to medical careers should be trained in "anatomy, surgery, chemistry, physiology, the preservation of health, [and] the properties of medicinal plants [as well as] midwifery." Toward the end of the century, a higher percentage of women from Utah studied medicine than from any other state or territory. Ellis Shipp left her four small children with another of her husband's wives while she studied at the Women's Medical College in Philadelphia in the 1870s. After a summer visit back home she became pregnant, but she returned to Philadelphia and delivered her fifth child the day after her last exam. When she returned home a doctor, she was part of a steady stream of eastern-trained female doctors who taught nursing and obstetrics in Salt Lake City to delegates from far-flung congregations. When these students returned home, they gave the classes to their communities. In the 1880s the women created a hospital in Salt Lake for medical treatment, maternity care, and training.

Through activities and meetings the Relief Society bound women together in friendship and spirituality. Mary Griffin, the Society's leader in the small town of Clarkston, Utah, wrote of her group of thirty sisters that "they speak words of comfort and encouragement to each other." Joseph Smith said in 1842 that the women would have "the privileges, blessings and gifts of the Priesthood," that "healing the sick, [and] casting out devils," would follow those with "virtuous life and conversation, and diligence in keeping all the commandments." Though not officially granted the priesthood, women frequently exercised these spiritual gifts.

The journals of early Mormon women are replete with accounts like Abigail Leonard's of miraculous healings. Once she told an afflicted woman's husband that he must "send for the sisters. The sisters came, washed, anointed, and administered to [prayed over] her. The patient's extremities were cold, her eyes set, a spot in the back apparently mortified [decayed], and [there was] every indication that death was upon her. But before the sisters had ceased to administer, the blood went coursing through her system." The patient's appetite returned, Leonard reported, and within three days she sat up and combed her hair.

Mormon women's worship took forms foreign to modern experience. In group meetings they spoke in strange languages, with their messages interpreted by others. Speaking in tongues was not uncommon within the Mormon community, although it was little encouraged or publicized. Fanny Stenhouse once reported a visitation in which one of Brigham Young's wives lit up with a supernatural glow. She placed her hands on Mrs. Stenhouse's head and poured out a flood of incomprehensible eloquence. At that, Mrs. Stenhouse reported, a thrill went through her body as if she had been "listening to an inspired seeress."

These spiritual experiences united women in a close sisterhood distinct from the home sphere and the congregation. In this sisterly society, the women shared both work and mystical moments, communing with heaven and believing in their own cooperative powers. As their publication the *Woman's Exponent* noted, "If the sisters would unite together, more of them, and concentrate their efforts systematically, they could almost do anything they wish to do in the right direction."

Another aspect of Mormonism that bound its women together was the practice of plural marriage, variously called polygamy, celestial marriage, or "the principle." In this notable doctrine, men in positions of leadership with sufficient incomes were encouraged, and even commanded, to marry more than one wife. Although it had been revealed to Joseph Smith in 1831, this radical doctrine was not publicly acknowledged until 1852 when the Saints had settled in Utah. Several years later, the Republican-controlled Congress moved to halt the practice.

This dismaying doctrine predictably caused major difficulties for the fledgling sect, shocking Mormons of both sexes. As John Taylor, later president of the church, reported, "I had always entertained strict ideas of virtue, and I felt as a married man that this was to me . . . an appalling thing to do. . . . Nothing but . . . the revelations of God . . . could have induced me to embrace such a principle as this." Brigham Young, who later married more than twenty wives, said, "I was not desirous of shrinking from any duty . . . but it was the first time in my life I had desired the grave." Many accounts of questioning and doubt remain, but some felt there was strong validity for the doctrine. Others complied merely as a religious duty, despite their feelings. Generally the first wives, facing the loss of their husbands' loyalty and affections, raged and wept—but then consented. Some even encouraged reluctant husbands. Both men and women came around to believing that celestial marriage was right. Many, like Mary Jane Done Jones, admitted that such a life was difficult. "Polygamy was a great trial to any woman. And it was just as hard on the man. He had to learn to adjust to his women and his troubles were made worse by the women having to learn to adjust too." Privately and among themselves the women admitted their problems with the practice, even as they publicly defended it.

Eliza R. Snow, Zion's most prominent woman poet and the Relief Society head, as genteel and refined an eastern lady as could be imagined, plurally married first Joseph Smith, then Brigham Young. She never regretted her marriages but considered the practice a "pure and holy principle, not only tending to individual purity and elevation of character, but also instrumental in producing a more perfect type of manhood mentally and physically." Augusta Joyce Crocheron thought that any woman could be a one and only wife, but that "it takes a great deal more Christian philosophy and fortitude and self-discipline to be a wife in this order of marriage." Those who chose to be second wives, she said, "casting out all selfishness," had attained "a height, a mental power, a spiritual plane" above others.

The revelation that Joseph Smith had been granted on plural marriage commanded him to follow the practices of the Old Testament leaders Abraham, Isaac, and Jacob, with no reasons being given. That lust was responsible for the direction seems unlikely. Although Joseph Smith was certainly married to many women, only one child from his multiple unions, besides his first with Emma, has ever been claimed. But if no reasons for following the practice were given, some benefits resulted. Polygamy provided homes for single immigrant women and others needing to establish family connections. More plural marriages took place in the near-famine times of 1856 and 1857, perhaps because well-to-do members were encouraged to care for women who needed help. Polygamy also provided extra hands to seek a living and gave Mormon husbands to women who might otherwise have had to marry out of the faith, although the Utah population included slightly more men than women. And the principle encouraged female independence and cooper-

The Relief Society, founded by Emma Smith in 1842, was disbanded during the Mormons' western movement. Eliza Snow (above) reestablished the Society in Utah in 1867.

Joseph F. Smith and family around 1901. He and his 6 wives had a total of 48 children.

ation with sister wives who divided up the labor. In a community where men were often away from home, women developed valuable skills. Finally, plural marriage, by making Mormons distinct from other Americans, strengthened the community's internal bonds as they defended themselves.

Of the polygamous men, very few had more than two or three wives. The most usual plural family was a middle-aged pair with a second, and maybe a third, younger wife. The number of those practicing polygamy differed widely over time and from place to place, but perhaps 9 percent of the adult male population were involved. Accurate figures are elusive, because many marriages were secretly performed and divorce was common. Young approved divorces for all of the women, and some of the men, who requested them. The system did not produce happier marriages or increase the population. Plural wives each had fewer children than monogamous wives, but the individual husbands had more offspring. Ideally, each wife had her own house and the husband divided his time among the different wives and houses. If the wives lived in one house, sisterly harmony sometimes prevailed, but at other times it did not, mostly due to financial inequality and jealousy. Brigham Young counseled Mormon women to concentrate on motherhood rather than romance, to rise above petty difficulties, and to think of their eternal happiness. Above all, Mormons stressed the practicalities of marriage. When the widowed midwife Patty Sessions married again, she confided, "I was married to John Parry and I feel to thank the Lord that I have some one to cut my wood for me."

Polygamy attracted national opposition to Mormonism and ensured that these people were not forgotten in the rest of the United States. The eastern press condemned them as a bad example of popular sovereignty, arguing that this is what might happen if the states and territories were allowed to decide such matters for themselves. If states could choose slavery, they could also practice an abomination like polygamy. The United States denied the Utah Territory's petitions for statehood in 1848, 1856, 1861, 1872, 1882, and 1887. Utahns wanted to control their own government, because as it was, their territorial laws could be overruled by national legislation, and the federal courts could move in on all local adjudications. California became a state in 1850, Nevada in 1864, but Utah, despite having met the population requirement many times over, remained a territory, a vast foreign enclave in the intermountain West. Political independence eluded the Mormons because polygamy, hostility to outside capitalism, and the power of their church made too many enemies.

In 1856 the Republican party platform included a resolution to prohibit in the territories those "twin relics of barbarism—Polygamy and Slavery," setting the United States and the Mormons of the desert kingdom on a collision course. In 1862 Congress passed the Morrill Anti-Bigamy Act, which levied penalties against plural marriage, disincorporated the Mormon church, and limited the value of the real estate the church could hold to $50,000. Any property valued above that figure could be confiscated. President Abraham Lincoln supported his party by signing the bill, but he did not enforce it, saying he would not harass the Mormons. He likened them to a log that was "too hard to split, too wet to burn, and too heavy to move." He plowed around such logs.

After the Civil War, with slavery eliminated, Congress attacked polygamy again. The Cullom Act, passed by the House of Representatives in 1870, provided that all prosecutions of plural marriages should be heard by federal judges and juries to assure a fair trial. When the news reached Utah, three thousand Mormon women assembled in the Salt Lake Tabernacle to demonstrate, protesting that Mormon practices were the "only reliable safeguard of female virtue and innocence" against "the fearful sin of prostitution." This political activism and female support for polygamy amazed the country, and the bill did not pass the Senate.

At this female mass meeting, the first of many, the women militantly and articulately defended themselves. In suffrage leader Sarah M. Kimball's introduction she said, "We have been driven from place to place, and wherefore? Simply for believing and practicing the counsels of God, as contained in the gospel of heaven." Eliza R. Snow noted that if Mormon women were the "stupid, degraded, heartbroken beings that we have been represented, silence might better become us." But, she went on, "As women of God, women fulfilling high and responsible positions, per-forming sacred duties—women who stand not as dictators, but as coun-selors to their husbands, and who, in the purest, noblest sense of refined womanhood, are truly helpmates—we not only speak because we have the right, but justice and humanity demand that we should." Mormon women thus entered the political sphere.

Mormon women surprised the nation by getting the vote. The *New York Times* had suggested that granting suffrage to women, enabling them to vote out polygamy, would solve the Utah problem. In 1870 the Utah legislature passed a bill allowing women to vote. Wyoming had passed such a bill the previous year, but by a quirk of timing the women of Utah became the first women to cast ballots in the nineteenth century. The Mormon women disappointed out-of-state observers by supporting polygamy.

John Coyner, a Presbyterian educator in the West, wrote in 1879 that he had once believed that Utah's women were held by their men in a "kind of captivity" that made them unable to "escape from their degradation." He had thought that the coming of the railroad would allow them to "gladly embrace the opportunity of escap[ing] thralldom. But, in this," he noted, he was "much mistaken."

Women of the Relief Society published the *Woman's Exponent,* an independent bimonthly newspaper, from 1872 to 1914. Frankly feminist in its orientation while devoted to the church, its subtitle read "The Rights of Women of Zion and the Rights of Women of all Nations." Women spoke for themselves in these pages and encouraged others to speak. "Girls don't be afraid of the term 'strong-minded,' for of such there is certainly a necessity," a column in 1875 cautioned. "The stronger you are in mind and body the better for you . . . do not wait for any other person to bring you forward." The paper proclaimed the equality of the sexes and urged equal pay for equal work as well as exercise, sensible clothing, and educational and professional advancement, all with church approval. Political work became church work.

The national suffrage leader Elizabeth Cady Stanton lectured in Salt Lake City in 1871, raising her voice above the constant wail of babies carried by their mothers. Stanton condemned polygamy but invited Mormon suffragists to conventions in the East. She and her colleague Susan B. Anthony at least tolerated and sometimes befriended the Mormon women. When the two eastern suffrage organizations, the National Woman Suffrage Association (NWSA) and the American Woman Suffrage Association (AWSA), discussed consolidation, Stanton insisted that all women with common goals be welcomed, including "Mormon women, black women, and Indian women," and she prevailed.

Susan B. Anthony, an advocate of women's suffrage, saw Mormon women as being in the vanguard of the movement because they already had the vote in Utah.

In 1900, when Mormon women attended Susan B. Anthony's eightieth birthday in Atlanta, they brought a dress length of black silk brocade from Utah. Anthony said her pleasure in the fabric was "quadrupled because it was made by women politically equal with men." It seems evident that the obedient Mormon women found no tension between their religious and political lives.

The mounting campaign against polygamy continued into the 1880s, supported by most Americans, the Protestant clergy, federal officials, and the press, which denounced the practice as evil, an abomination, a stigma, a practice that degraded and enslaved women. Many sensational and humorous anecdotes appeared in print. Mark Twain, for instance, in his book *Roughing It,* noted that he had gone west planning to reform polygamy. But when he saw the women, he was touched. His heart warmed toward the "poor, ungainly, and pathetically 'homely' creatures." He had to turn away to conceal the "generous moisture" in his eyes. He concluded that "the man that marries one of them has done an act of Christian charity which entitles him to the kindly applause of mankind, not their harsh censure—and the man that marries sixty of them has done a deed of openhanded generosity so sublime that the nation should stand uncovered in his presence and worship in silence!"

The Mormons, meanwhile, felt they were only practicing their religion and that polygamy was necessary for salvation. Hostile federal legislation steadily cut away their base. In 1882, the Edmunds Act sent a commission from Washington to take over the territorial government. The act punished polygamy by a three-hundred-dollar fine or six months in jail. Local federal officials disenfranchised all who believed in polygamy, whether they were practicing it or not, thereby excluding some twelve thousand men and women from registering and voting. The Mormons appealed this law to the Supreme Court, but the appeal was denied.

Polygamy per se was difficult to prove, so suspects were tried instead for "unlawful cohabitation," resulting in 1,004 convictions between 1884 and 1893, with 31 more convictions for polygamy itself. Amos Milton Mussner, who served time in prison for polygamy, commented on "this

charming abode, with its service of striped clothing, decayed vegetables, maggotty meats, and sodden bread." The number of convictions would no doubt have been higher if many people had not simply disappeared from view, avoiding the law in an "underground" of safehouses and hiding places. Federal marshals chased after, tracked down, and hunted the "cohabs." Women also took flight into the underground, hiding evidence of pregnancy and giving birth to unnamed children under the most trying circumstances. Church affairs slowed to a halt during the raids, with most leaders in jail or in hiding. Still, the Mormons did not capitulate.

In 1887, the Edmunds-Tucker Act amended and enforced the 1862 law and got really tough. Plural wives were now forced to testify against their husbands. The corporation of the church, the Perpetual Emigration Fund, and the Nauvoo Legion were all dissolved, and all church property was confiscated to benefit district schools. All the children from plural

Because they considered themselves the victims of unjust persecution, Mormon men who were jailed for polygamy wore their uniforms as a badge of pride.

Martha Hughes Cannon, a physician, state senator, and plural wife, claimed that she was no slave to her husband. "If her husband has four wives," she said, "she has three weeks of freedom every month."

marriages were disinherited, and all Mormon participation in government was forbidden. The act also abolished Utah's seventeen-year-old woman suffrage legislation, thus excluding all the women voters in Utah, whether Mormons or not, married or single. The Supreme Court upheld this law.

Now completely crippled, with no hope of judicial redress, the Church of Jesus Christ of Latter-day Saints sacrificed its practice of plural marriage to preserve the church's life. Wilford Woodruff, the church's president in 1890 and a member of it almost since its beginning, wrote in his journal that he acted for the "temporal salvation of the church." In a document he called the Manifesto he proclaimed polygamy at an end. As he wrote, "Inasmuch as laws have been enacted by Congress forbidding plural marriages, which laws have been pronounced constitutional by the court of last resort, I hereby declare my intention to submit to those laws, and to use my influence with the members of the Church over which I preside to have them do likewise."

The reading of the Manifesto at the general conference meeting stunned the congregation, which nonetheless unanimously approved it. One of Samuel Spalding's plural wives described the scene: "I was there in the tabernacle the day of the Manifesto, and I tell you it was an awful feeling. There Pres. Woodruff read the Manifesto that made me no longer a wife and might make me homeless. . . . But I voted for it because it was the only thing to do." Most husbands continued to support their polygamous families, but many stopped living with them. Some moved their families to Canada or Mexico, where plural marriage was not prosecuted. Yet, other Mormons, believing the Manifesto to be a temporary expedient, quietly contracted even more plural marriages. A second manifesto in 1904 prohibited further plural marriages, threatening the offenders with excommunication.

With the 1890 Manifesto and the official ending of plural marriage came a relaxation of prosecution and persecution for the Mormons. The Manifesto turned out to be the price paid for statehood, which finally came in 1896. The Utahns, freed from Washington's supervision, embraced home rule.

Woman suffrage was restored. Utah entered the Union as only the third state to have it, twenty-four years before the Nineteenth Amendment to the Constitution extended that right throughout the nation. In the first election after suffrage was extended, in 1895, Dr. Martha Hughes Cannon became the first woman in the United States to be elected a state senator, having defeated her husband, among others; two women were elected that year to the Utah House.

Another woman elected to the Utah House of Representatives, Alice Merrill Horne, was born in a log cabin in Fillmore, Utah in 1868, the fourth child of 14. Her father married two other wives who had additional children. She learned about nature and singing from her father, about dramatics and handwork from her mother.

In 1876, when she was eight, Alice moved from rural Fillmore to Salt Lake City to live with her widowed grandmother Bathsheba Smith, a feminist leader who had made the original motion to grant Utah women the right to vote in 1870, and who led the Relief Society after 1901. In Salt Lake City she met leaders of consequence and learned about painting and architecture. She studied art and literature at the University of Deseret, earning a teaching certificate.

Indignant at an art curriculum adopted by the Salt Lake City schools, one that emphasized mechanical rather than aesthetic principles, Alice moved into politics. She managed the campaign of Oscar W. Moyle who worked to supplant the system.

She was elected a state representative herself in 1898. At the nominating convention, a gentleman said, "I know a good looking young woman

Always active, Alice Merrill Horne, the second woman elected to the Utah House of Representatives, began writing her memoirs in 1948 at age 80.

who works like hell, who will run like a deer, and her name is Alice Merrill Horne!" Horne credited her beautiful "hand-made clothes" for her election over some highly intelligent, but dowdy, women. She said she wished she could sew herself some brains, but despite her modesty she set to work and distinguished herself in public health, educating school teachers, and promoting public art. She introduced measures to protect fish and game and to award college scholarships for prospective teachers. She encouraged artists, put on exhibitions, and collected art for the state. She sponsored the bill creating the Utah Intitute of Fine Arts which established the WPA Orchestra, later the Utah Symphony. Despite her humble beginnings, the daughter of pioneers, she was determined, even aggressive, in working toward educational and artistic goals.

These pioneer Mormon women, daughters of New England and the Middle West, emigrants from the British Isles and Scandinavia, were very much like other women of their time, but their allegiance to the faith led them in new directions. The loneliness of other pioneer settlements did not affect these women, who lived in groups, and they escaped the false limitations of class differences and polite society in the East. Primarily working-class and domestic women, they managed homes and raised children. They had sacrificed much to join an outcast sect, but their religion brought them comfort and peace. They followed their church leaders out of conviction and faith. In a frontier community with scant professional resources, women moved into positions of social, cultural, and educational leadership, cooperating to help each other and save money. Their native gifts were encouraged for the benefit of the community, and imagination and initiative brought them accomplishment and social recognition.

The practice of plural marriage distanced Mormon women from the rest of society, but even while acknowledging the personal cost of it, some women turned it to their benefit, finding men to marry, cooperating for freedom from some kinds of household work, developing independence, and adding to their household's income.

The oppression of their group led many women to political involvement, and with the encouragement of church leaders they congregated, organized, wrote, and voted in support of themselves and their way of life. In one of the neatest ironic contradictions of the period, the women of Utah became effective early feminists.

Chapter 7

Mormons in the Nation, 1890–1945

T he Church of Jesus Christ of Latter-day Saints holds the doctrine of the separation of church and state; the non-interference of church authority in political matters; and the absolute freedom and independence of the individual in the performance of his political duties.

—Address to the World by the First Presidency (1907)

The end of polygamy and Utah's admission to the Union marked a turning point in Mormon history. While they clung stubbornly to their "peculiar principle," the Mormons remained an isolated and alienated people. After losing the polygamy battle, the church's members moved toward integration with their fellow citizens. As their fortress mentality slowly dissolved, Mormons became good Americans.

Soon after statehood, the Mormons adopted national economic and political patterns. While polygamy had symbolized the difference between Mormons and others, it was their economic policies that most galled outsiders. Their cooperative movement had been based on communal action, simplicity in consumption, and self-sufficiency, but outsiders saw instead monopoly and protectionism, and resented the church's interference with competition and a free market. All that changed, however, until by 1914 most Salt Lake City banks and department stores, the best residential property, and all the skyscrapers were owned or controlled by non-Mormon interests.

This co-operative store is bedecked with banners celebrating Utah's admittance to the union in 1896.

The Mormons, once isolated, now became capitalistic, conservative, pro-American individualists. Once hated and feared, these religious rebels moved steadily toward acceptance. The Mormon church welcomed visitors to Temple Square with public organ recitals and Tabernacle Choir concerts. As the hard work and high morals of church members began to draw praise, positive articles about them began to appear in general periodicals.

But after losing much of its uniqueness to assimilation, the church now reemphasized the differences that set its members apart from the American norm, such as tithing and the Word of Wisdom—the church's dietary code. The church also gave new attention to genealogy, temple attendance, and baptism for the dead. In the 1930s the welfare program helped church members who were in need. Mormonism became a distinctive religious community within the larger American community, instead of a community in itself.

Tithing, the old law requiring Mormons to pay one tenth of their incomes to the church, was revived by Lorenzo Snow, the church president who had succeeded Wilford Woodruff in 1898. Aghast at the heavy debt burden—nearly $2 million—accumulated from the conflict with the U.S. government, Snow initiated a program of business retrenchment, giving up church control of mining and railroad interests. To raise money to pay the debt, Snow dramatically reintroduced the tithing program, when visiting poor, drought-stricken St. George, Utah, in 1899. There he promised the Saints that if they would pay their full tithing, the Lord would "open the windows of heaven" and bless them. They paid their tithing, and St. George got its rain and a fairly good harvest. From then on, President Snow campaigned to revive the tithing principle.

Tithing's revenues increased sufficiently to pay off the church's debts by 1907. To this day, the annual tithe of one tenth of their income from faithful members pays for the construction and upkeep of Mormon chapels all over the world, supports church schools, and covers all congregational expenses. Tithing, far in excess of business income, provides the church's major revenue.

Many members believe that paying one's tithing improves their financial situation. One young man, David Perkins, recently noted that he had become a great believer in tithing. "Tithing has always been tough. I knew it was ideally necessary, but realistically I didn't think it was possible." When his family went through some hard financial times, he "had to exercise a great deal of faith to pay [his] tithing. I don't know how we got through that. I don't think I'm supposed to know, but I think I'm supposed to remember that it took faith."

The Word of Wisdom, a set of dietary regulations, has taken on new importance for defining Mormon orthodoxy. Originating in a revelation to Joseph Smith in 1833 at a time of temperance and health reform, the Word of Wisdom promised physical and intellectual strength to those who refused alcohol, tobacco, and "hot drinks," interpreted as tea and coffee. The Word of Wisdom was practiced only sporadically in the nineteenth century. Faithful Mormons now generally do not smoke or drink alcohol, and adherence to these dietary rules still sets Latter-day Saints apart.

At statehood, Utah voters divided themselves into the two national political parties, the Democrats and Republicans, although the Republicans have generally predominated. Nevertheless, this division did not quiet suspicions about church political influence or remove the taint of polygamy. Some Americans doubted whether Mormon church leaders should be allowed to hold political office at all. When B. H. Roberts, a church official with three wives, was elected to the U.S. House of Representatives in 1898, a torrent of negative petitions flooded Congress from all over the nation, many from women's groups lobbying for a con-

B. H. Roberts, elected to the U.S. House of Representatives in 1898, was denied a seat because he practiced polygamy. Most government officials did not insist that long-standing plural marriages be broken up after polygamy ended in 1890, but Roberts' election stirred up old animosities.

Reed Smoot, member of the Twelve Apostles and not a polygamist, was elected to the U.S. Senate in 1902. Although seated initially, popular indignation forced the Senate to undertake a lengthy investigation of the church that finally resulted in Smoot's vindication.

stitutional amendment prohibiting polygamy. A House committee overwhelmingly denied Roberts his seat.

When Utahns elected Reed Smoot, a church leader with one wife, to the U.S. Senate in 1903, his election was opposed by non-Mormon Salt Lake City businessmen, lawyers, and ministers who sent a formal protest to Washington. More than 4 million signatures were gathered against Smoot from around the nation. Again women's groups were heavily involved. What followed was a long and thorough investigation of the church in a Senate hearing. Once more the complaint was the church-state issue. Could Smoot, a member of a self-perpetuating religious body, fairly represent the temporal affairs of the state, or would he be ruled by his Mormon beliefs? The commission voted against Smoot, although the minority found that the church had divorced itself from politics after 1890, but the Senate voted in his favor. After a private meeting, President Theodore Roosevelt supported Smoot, who served for thirty years.

Many feared that the Mormons would not really give up plural marriage. This supposition, kept alive in the press, was what was really behind the disapproval of Mormons in office. Some Mormons did hold to polygamy. Sensing a conflict between church doctrine and practice, they contracted new marital unions and accepted the excommunication that came with them. Indeed, many fundamentalist Mormons preferred excommunication to renouncing polygamy, which they considered central to the church's teachings. Others, who accepted the ban, dreaded the discussion of plural marriage which had become an embarrassment. The social and political fallout from polygamy dogged the church for years. The politics of the practice was eventually secularized, but the process took four decades.

One of the things that helped to break down old prejudices was Mormon support for the American cause in World War I. Initially, the Red Cross hesitated to cooperate with the Relief Society, a sectarian organization, but finally recognized it as the only access to Utah. Eventually more than one thousand local units of the Relief Society became Red Cross auxiliaries. In addition, Mormons enlisted in the armed forces in generous numbers, and Utah pledged well above its quota of financial support to the war effort by buying government bonds. This support of the nation at war was a major help in changing the national image of the church. The church has always opposed war in general, but it encourages citizens to answer the call of the constitutional government in any country.

The Great Depression of the 1930s hit the economies of Utah and its bordering states very hard. Unemployment climbed to more than 25 percent. As many people faced bankruptcy, the Mormon church began local programs for the destitute. Its members helped each other find jobs, shared food, set up farms, and recycled clothing, always making an effort to keep people at useful work and avoiding the simple distribution of money, the dreaded "dole."

In 1936 the church systematized and extended its social programs, taking over the Relief Society's social welfare activities to include employment in church-operated enterprises and distribution of food and clothing

Though instituted to help church members during the Depression, Mormon relief activities continue to the present. This store was photographed in 1941.

Lorenzo Snow became president of the church in 1898 at the age of 84. He was the last church president to have known Joseph Smith personally.

to families from a chain of storehouses. All church members helped, with projects overseen by local ward (congregational) leadership. Church president Heber J. Grant described the program's purposes as doing away with "the curse of idleness" and establishing the principles of "independence, industry, thrift, and self-respect." This Church Welfare Plan, as it came to be called, helped members who would otherwise be dependent on government aid. Each congregation maintained a work project, hiring the unemployed and paying them from credit established at the storehouse. Communities grew food on vacant lots. Some thirty thousand people received aid, and by 1938 about twenty-two thousand church members were off the federal relief rolls, though many still remained.

The Church Welfare Plan continues today, extending the church's early strain of cooperation and self-sufficiency. Members continue to contribute their "fast offerings," the cost of two meals monthly, for the relief of the poor, as well as to work at welfare farms, to preserve food at church canning factories, and to distribute goods to those in either temporary or long-term need. Besides this general preparation, each family is encouraged to store enough food, water, and clothing for a year against need or disaster. At times of flood, fire, or earthquake the church organizes volunteer labor to mount relief efforts and dispatches supplies all over the world.

In another effort to help members care for themselves, the church reversed the "gathering" plan, wherein converts were encouraged to emigrate to the central home of the church, and instead encouraged converts to remain in their own countries, even though zealous missionary work in America and abroad continued. In 1899 President Lorenzo Snow recommended that converts no longer emigrate to Utah. The rate of immigration consequently slowed drastically even as the church grew throughout the world. Joseph F. Smith, the first church president to travel outside the country while in office, carried this message abroad as he traveled in 1904 and 1910 to meet with members and missionaries.

A few new colonies were planted for economic expansion: in the Big Horn Basin of Wyoming; in Alberta, Canada; in Oregon, and in southern Arizona. But most Mormons who left the state went on their own. Typically, the little Mormon villages had ten or fifteen years of hard pioneering, followed by twenty or thirty prime years when the town's fine houses and public buildings were constructed. Then the villages reached the limits that their watered land could maintain and the young people had to move away to find jobs. The emigration stream went first to the West Coast, then throughout the nation, building up congregations wherever it deposited members.

Rather than a single bastion against the world, the Mormon culture developed a heartland, the Zion of Utah, and a periphery, made up of settlements in cities elsewhere. In 1922 George W. McCune of Ogden, Utah, was sent to Los Angeles to head the first cluster of congregations there. By 1927 some twenty thousand Latter-day Saints lived in California, and by 1929 there were two stakes, or dioceses, in Los Angeles, each with eight to ten wards, or congregations. ("Stake" is a biblical name referring to a peg holding up the tent of Zion.) That was a small number among the total of one thousand wards, in 104 stakes, mostly in Utah, Arizona, and Idaho, but the California stakes marked a trend. In 1934 the New York Saints organized a stake, after which periphery stakes multiplied throughout the nation.

Many Mormons were uneasy at the idea of dispersion, hating to expose their children to the temptations of an evil world. They feared that their offspring might be lost from the faith, drawn by secular interests. But the dry alkaline lands of Utah could not support the ever-increasing Mormon population in anything but poverty. As a matter of necessity, the young people set off into the world.

Young people who had grown up barefoot on Utah farms crossed the western mountains to California, where they found buckets of golden oranges for sale on every corner. Boys who learned diligence in thinning sugar beets adapted to blue- and white-collar jobs. They built tidy

California bungalows, marveling at hot and cold running water. As they joined the middle class they remembered the old days of privation.

This outmigration shaped the twentieth-century church. This newly national church now had to meet the needs of a dispersed population. As part of its program, the church emphasized early teaching, to develop strong Mormon identities. Carol Potter, a mother of four young children, voiced the concern that led to these programs. "I want [my children] to be active in the church and to have strong testimonies of the gospel. I'm afraid because of the world. You never know what the outside influences are. All you can do is pray for [the children]. You can teach them, but really all you can do is pray." An elaborate pattern of organization, one that involved its members in many activities, became a hallmark of Mormon life. Special organizations within the church addressed the needs of different age groups. The Relief Society had long served women, and the Sunday School program provided Sunday religious instruction to members of all ages. The Young Women's and Young Men's Mutual Improvement Associations ran cultural, religious, and recreational activities for young people over twelve, and the Primary Association held weekly religious and recreational instruction for children. All but the Sunday School met regularly on weekdays and evenings, and held many extra special events.

In order to help young people keep up their Mormon lives, the individual wards sponsored a lively cultural program: an unending succession of three-act plays, speech festivals, dance instruction, musical concerts, sporting events, and field trips that united the young people in social activities. These programs aimed to improve individual talents while helping the young people develop close friends. One San Francisco sailor who joined the church after attending such events, testified that he had been converted "by girls and dances." Underlying this all was the hope that young people would find Mormon husbands and wives rather than be lost in the larger population. Active Mormons who had children of various ages might very well find themselves at the chapel every day of the week.

Karl McCord, an adult leader with his hair still painted white for his role as Benjamin Franklin in an original short play, once mused, "I wonder if there's any other place where just anybody who wanted to perform—young people and older people—could." He had been impressed by these shows when considering joining the church. "We take it for granted," he said, that every congregation can put on these shows, "but it is a marvelous thing to me."

The church developed elaborate record-keeping methods to monitor members' activity. Small-town boys and girls were not to drop out of sight and never be found again. The auxiliaries steadily moved toward greater centralization under churchwide leadership as the church dispersed. For the migrants who left Utah to go out to the periphery, the church served as their primary community, to which many clung as to a lifeline.

Schools served the same purpose of bringing together the young people of the church. In early Utah, a wide-ranging school system had been developed to meet the needs of the Mormon settlements. With statehood, this system shrank after 1896, but it was adapted to serve the broader church population. Shortly before statehood, public schools had replaced the local church schools. The church gradually closed or turned over to local jurisdictions its thirty-four high-school-level academies that had once been the backbone of the church educational system from Chihuahua, Mexico, to Alberta, Canada. In recent times the church's policy has been to organize schools wherever other systems are nonexistent, seriously deficient, or inaccessible to members, then to discontinue them when they are no longer needed.

As the older educational system closed down, a new one began. The church substantially enlarged Brigham Young University and several other of its colleges. Since not all Mormons were able to attend these schools, the church opened institutes of religion at many other colleges, featuring just religion classes to teach their students and promote social cohesion.

Brigham Young University was located in Utah, but other important church institutions have been widely dispersed, temples for example.

As part of the 50th
anniversary of Brigham
Young University in 1925, a
parade passes before the
Karl G. Maeser Memorial
Building.

After forty years of construction, the grand Salt Lake temple was completed in 1893, the fourth temple built in Utah. Temples have been built continuously since then around the globe, until sixty-two temples now are available to conduct regular sessions or are in the process of construction, and plans exist to double that number. These temples are built in many architectural styles, with some like bastions, others in the prairie style, some with central spires, and two that are round. The Los Angeles temple, built in 1956, was then the largest. The 1974 Washington, D.C., temple built in suburban Silver Spring, Maryland, echoes the Salt Lake temple with its six towers. Early European temples were small and modest.

These temples, which are in fact not for congregational gathering, serve a unique LDS doctrinal function: to redeem the dead by performing ceremonies for these ancestors. The Latter-day Saints identify their family members through genealogical research. The Saints go to the temples where temple workers baptize and marry them for their ancestors by proxy. As Joseph Smith described this process, Mormons "seal those who dwell on earth to those who dwell in heaven" and "redeem our dead, and connect ourselves with our fathers which are in heaven."

The Mormons believe that everyone who has ever lived should be able to accept or reject the gospel of Jesus Christ. Through temple rituals, the family connections of earthly life are extended into eternity. Mormons believe that people who have died can choose whether or not to accept the temple work done for them. A biblical justification for this procedure is found in the writings of Paul: "Else what shall they do which are baptized for the dead, if the dead rise not at all? Why are they then baptized for the dead" (I Corinthians 15:29).

Mormon temple ceremonies include baptism for the dead, washing and anointing, endowments, and marriages (sealings) for eternity. An endowment leads a person through the Plan of Salvation toward a Christlike life; in this ceremony, participants make solemn promises that they do not discuss outside the temple.

A Mormon first participates in endowment ceremonies for himself, usually before going on a mission or prior to marriage "for time and all eternity." After a person's own endowment, he or she performs vicarious endowments, going through the temple for someone else who has not had the opportunity. Members are encouraged to return often for endowment services.

Going through a separate temple ceremony lasting several hours for every person who has ever lived on earth is a staggering undertaking. Joseph Smith once estimated that a thousand years might be required to complete the task. As of 1991, temple work had been completed for more than 113 million individuals.

The church invites the public to visit its new temples before the dedication ceremonies are held for them. After that, only the faithful members—those who have been baptized and confirmed and recommended by their local leaders—may enter the temple. One's templeworthiness is judged by annual private personal interviews with the bishop and the "stake" president.

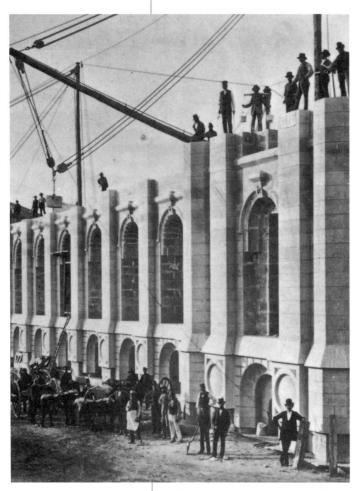

A vast Family History Program supplies the names for the vicarious endowments. Members research their own ancestry and do the temple work for them. Meanwhile, traveling teams microfilm records all over the world. As volunteers extract names, dates, and relationships, the library reconstitutes families. Since 1938, Mormons have gathered vital statistics for some 8 billion names from more than a hundred countries.

These records lie in a huge vault carved into a granite cliff in a Utah canyon. In this dim interior, with its controlled temperature and humidity, are gathered the documents of the Family History Library, where it is hoped they will last forever. Meanwhile, copies of these tremendous genealogical resources— 1,970,452 rolls of microfilm in 1993—can be borrowed from the Salt Lake City headquarters by members and nonmembers alike all over the world.

The Salt Lake Temple, dedicated in 1893, took 40 years and $4 million to build. The temple under construction is shown above; the dome of the state capitol shows through the spires of the finished temple (opposite page).

David Staley, a volunteer in a local library, talks of his fascination with the records. "When I'm reading the microfilms, sometimes, a spirit takes over and I feel very close to these people." He likes to find out "how they earned their living and a little about their trials and tribulations." Many Mormons are fascinated by geneology.

Although they were humbled by national governmental power at the turn of the century, the Mormons have steadily accommodated themselves to national norms. A new flexibility in church policies regarding politics, economics, and marriage has helped to lessen tensions between

them and their other American neighbors as they have adapted to the modern world. They have also won a degree of public admiration, especially for their cultural activities and Welfare Plan, easing still further the tensions with the outside world.

After World War I, the Mormons' growing membership spilled beyond the borders of their old desert kingdom to the cities of the United States. New congregations sprang up all over the country, increasingly housed in attractive buildings. Far from wasting away, the church proved stronger than ever. America's indigenous religion had come of age not as a bizarre remnant of a bygone era but as an effective religious organization with beliefs and practices that met the needs of modern life yet set the Mormons apart from the population at large.

Chapter 8

The Church Since 1945

No unhallowed hand can stop the work from progressing; persecutions may rage, mobs may combine, armies may assemble, calumny may defame, but the truth of God will go forth boldly, nobly, and independent, till it has penetrated every continent, visited every clime, swept every country, and sounded in every ear, till the purposes of God shall be accomplished and the great Jehovah shall say the work is done.

—Joseph Smith, Jr., *The Wentworth Letter*, 1842

A typical Mormon family today is likely to be young and urban, with one more child than the people next door. The man may hold any sort of job, the woman may be slightly more likely to be at home than others in her neighborhood, although at 67 percent more Utah women are employed than the national average. About a third of the church's members are single, never married, divorced, or widowed. Many will be older than the general population, as healthy Mormons live an average of ten years longer than other Americans.

The family will live in a ward, the basic congregational unit, with two hundred to eight hundred members under the direction of a bishop and two counselors. The bishop feels a direct, personal responsibility for the people in his ward and oversees their religious and social activities. But he is not a trained professional like most pastors and priests. He is selected

This quilt was created to celebrate the 150th anniversary of the organization of the church of Latter-day Saints. The individual blocks depict scenes from church members' lives, such as temple marriage, family home evening, missionary work, and welfare, as well as several temples.

from the ward members to serve for three or four years while still engaged in his regular employment. After that he is released and someone else is chosen. To carry out a ward's full program, with its officers and teachers, musicians, sports specialists, nursery leaders, and home teachers, some two hundred people must accept voluntary church assignments.

A typical week for a Mormon family begins with a three-hour block of meetings every Sunday morning, with additional meetings before and after. Ward members join for Sacrament Meeting, the LDS worship service, and later, separate meetings for children, teenagers, and adults.

Despite much congregational activity, the church stresses that children should be taught the gospel's principles at home in family worship, which includes the blessing of food at meals and family prayer in the morning and evening. Family members gather one evening a week at Family Home Evening, when no other church programs can be scheduled, for gospel teaching and social activity. The church's members aim to develop a faith strong enough to withstand the reverses and temptations of daily life.

Several wards make up a stake, or diocese, to which each family also belongs. A stake will have from two thousand to seven thousand members. Each stake, presided over by a president and two counselors and also by a high council of twelve men, all unpaid, provides the church's full range of programs, including social services, employment assistance, and family history libraries as well as larger social activities. About one hundred people administer these programs, all part-time lay workers. No stake or ward officer receives compensation.

Women carry out a majority of these assignments, completely running the Relief Society, the Young Women's organization, the children's Primary organization, and filling most teaching positions. Some posts seem to demand unending time and concern. Sally Thompson loved her time as Relief Society president in New York City because she came to love so many women, many of them young mothers with husbands in school like her. She also loved the members' diversity, gaining an appreciation for many people, but she never felt that she could do all that she should. As an exhausted Relief Society president was once told, "They call it the Relief Society because it's such a relief when it's over."

Mormon women do not preside over congregations or become general authorities. Mormons consider men and women equal in status but to have different roles. Ideally, men support their families. While women are encouraged to earn college degrees, develop their talents, and contribute to their communities, they also devote themselves to family, motherhood, home, and church work. Women accomplish a great deal, but quietly. Historian and author Juanita Brooks, an excellent housekeeper and the mother of many, kept her ironing board set up in the living room with a couple of shirts out that needed to be ironed. She typed on her current project until someone came to visit. Then she covered the typewriter, plugged in the iron, opened the door, and ironed shirts while visiting. When the visitor left, she went back to the typewriter. Although her husband supported the family, the money she received for her published articles bought welcome extras.

Young lay members of the priesthood prepare bread and water for the sacrament (communion) during church services.

High school students daily attend an additional hour of a seminary scripture class. These classes are held at 6:00 or 6:30 a.m. and, with after-school sports, jobs, and homework, the students are very busy. An active young person may spend fifteen hours a week at church-related functions.

Special meetings, counseling, and visiting add church time to the schedules of many members. The relentless demands on their time, money, and energy are too much for some, who withdraw from active membership. As Tim Riordan, a ward member, left his house one night, he was surprised to hear his wife Geraldine yell down, "I hate you. I hate the church. And I hate you going out as much as you do." At first he did not understand her dismay at sitting home with three little children while he was off doing church work, but he cut down his time out to save his marriage and both are still active. The percentage of contemporary baptized Mormons who are currently disaffected from the church runs somewhere from 20 to 50 percent. Randy Lawton, who was assigned to ask people why they stopped coming to church in one area, assembled this composite answer: "I couldn't be a perfect Mormon, so I didn't feel as if I belonged there. I couldn't pay my tithing every month. I didn't feel as if I could take the sacrament every Sunday. I didn't agree with that [Sunday School] teacher. At times I didn't feel that I had the spirit of the Holy Ghost with me. I didn't feel I was in tune with what the home teachers were saying when they came and presented a program. When somebody called me to do something, I didn't respond with the degree of perfection that was expected. I can't walk on water for you people, and I don't hear trumpets every morning."

The teachings of high moral behavior sometimes lead to feelings of guilt. Not all families are ideal and many feel inadequate, sensing the real or imagined judgments of others. Some women feel guilty about working, others about staying home. With psychological problems similar to those of the larger population, adults break their promises and young people wander from the faith. While praising the family unit, the church acknowledges many problems. The present teaching reflects high standards as well as a failure to achieve them. Lessons for all ages emphasize family gentleness, kindness, and mutual respect. Mormons, however, admit to and condemn mistreatment in family situations and congregations.

Mormon couples marry earlier than members of the general population. They preach premarital chastity and honor marital fidelity, with most disapproving of any sexual intercourse outside of marriage. The overall divorce rate among all Mormons is only slightly below the national average, but for those married in Mormon temples divorce is at a lower rate.

Utah, with its 70 percent Mormon population, has the highest fertility rate in the nation, but not all Mormon families are large, and the birthrate in Utah rises and falls with national averages. Mormons use birth control, but not as soon or as frequently as others. In the general population, large family size tends toward coercive discipline and abuse. Mormon family relationships show, however, an increase of affection in larger families.

The teenagers of the typical Mormon family report lower rates of premarital sexual experience and teenage pregnancy than the national average. The rate of teenage childbirth is fairly high, however, because leaders discourage abortion and encourage pregnant girls to bear their babies and put them up for adoption.

In another program to extend family feeling, men are assigned to several families as home teachers, and women visit other women as visiting teachers. They visit monthly to befriend and help those in need. The visiting teacher may assist in times of sickness or with new babies, perhaps bringing in meals and offering advice. The home teacher might help move the family or paint the house, as well as assisting in emergencies. Warm friendships develop as members love their neighbors, although neighbors have been known to complain about visits from smiling Mormons with their "darned loaves of bread and plates of cookies."

Mormons value education. Joseph Smith believed in teaching the people correct principles and letting them govern themselves. He noted that "a man is saved no faster than he gains knowledge," and "the glory of God is intelligence." Mormons finish high school and college and attend graduate school at a higher rate than other groups. And their educational achievement level tends to correlate with church activity— the higher one's educational degree, the greater the likelihood of church involvement.

One place where commitment can be measured is during the testimony meeting on the first Sunday of each month, when members stand to speak from their hearts and "bear their testimonies," usually after fasting for two meals. Any member may address the congregation. He or she might say that he knows the church is true, that it was restored to the earth by Jesus Christ in these latter days, and that Joseph Smith is a prophet of God. Some speakers add faith-promoting experiences, stories, and thoughts about scripture. The members who have spoken or listened renew their commitment to live in a Christlike manner.

The Book of Mormon, which has been translated into more than 50 languages, is one of the most widely circulated books in the world. More than 88 million copies have been printed.

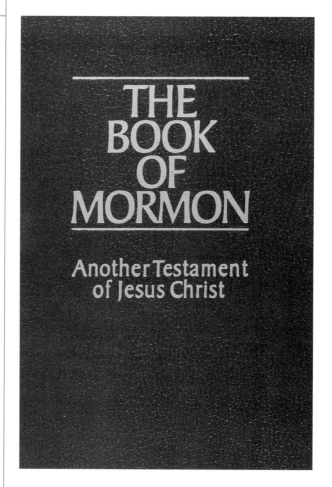

The ward bishop does not often preach sermons. Adults and young people twelve and older speak at meetings, using scriptural texts or other topics for their subjects. This training, practice, and indoctrination are what make Mormons a believing people in an unbelieving world.

Most Mormon families have little to do with the massive administrative structure headquartered in Salt Lake City, although they hear from the "general authorities" twice annually in televised conferences. These leaders oversee the worldwide operation of the church. The president, also called the Prophet, Seer, and Revelator, succeeds to that office from being the senior member of the Quorum of the Twelve Apostles. The president chooses two counselors from this group to form the First

Presidency of the church and names new members to the Quorum as openings occur. These leaders are approved by the members in an open meeting, but they are not elected, as no other candidates compete. The general authorities form a monolithic body: when the leaders speak, they speak as one, not as representatives of factions or points of view. Any debate or discussion goes on behind the scenes.

These general authorities, who are full-time leaders supported by church funds, have no ministerial training. Before their appointments, they usually have normal outside careers while serving voluntarily in church offices in the wards and stakes. When called as apostles, they serve until death. The apostles tend to be in their sixties, seventies, and eighties, and as seniority and length of service are required, the president is often an old man who is sometimes in poor health. Still, these leaders often show remarkable vigor, rising to the challenge of administering a huge operation. Each succeeding president stamps the church with his unique style. At this top level an extensive paid bureaucracy assists in such widespread functions as education, building construction, legal affairs, communications, and accounting.

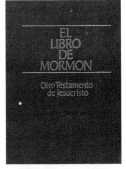

Mormons believe in the Old and New Testaments of the Bible, and that their church is a latter-day restoration of the teachings of Jesus Christ. They consider themselves Christians, believing in continued revelation from God. Mormons believe that the current president of the church communicates with the deity.

Besides the Bible, Mormons have three other books of scripture: The Book of Mormon, The Doctrine and Covenants, and The Pearl of Great Price. If the Book of Mormon is a book of ancient scripture, the Doctrine and Covenants is a work of modern scripture, mostly received as revelations to Joseph Smith. This scripture, divided into sections and verses, provides direction for the governance of the church in modern times. Although the book is open for expansion, Joseph Smith received 133 of the 138 sections in the book. These written revelations answer specific prayerful requests, but they also have universal application and can be used in the direction of individual lives.

The final book of scripture is the Pearl of Great Price, a collection of several short works, including ancient scriptures about Moses and Abraham, Joseph Smith's story of his early visions, and the Articles of Faith. The Mormons' wide array of scriptural works, and their unique manner of collecting scripture through revelation set them apart from other Christian churches, even though the contents of the Mormon scriptures are all deeply Christian.

Mormons have believed in teaching the gospel to others by missionary work since the beginning. Joseph Smith's youngest brother, Samuel, served one of the first missions two months after he was baptized in 1830, distributing the Book of Mormon around Palmyra, New York. He gave away books that brought Mormon stalwarts Brigham Young and Heber C. Kimball into the church. Since then, missionaries have traveled to most places in the world. In the early days, men set off on missions even when poor, hungry, and sick, often without money and leaving families behind, frequently for years at a time. Their wives supported the children with farming, handwork, school teaching, domestic or shop work, sending money to distant husbands as they could. The steady determination of the missionaries and the new members they have brought in have given the church its vigor over the years.

Often the missionaries were untrained farm boys who journeyed to countries where they were ignorant of the language and customs, frequently meeting with resistance and sometimes violence. Some have been attacked and beaten; several have been killed. Joseph Standing, on a mission to Georgia in 1879, was shot to death by a mob. A mob leader informed him, "The Government of the United States is against you, and there is no law in Georgia for Mormons," before shooting and killing him. Three men were arrested and positively identified before they were acquitted for the murder. Standing was the first Mormon missionary killed, but there have been others. In 1884, another mob interrupted church services held in a home in Cane Creek, Tennessee, demanding the surrender of the elders. Five people died in the gunfire. An elder in disguise went to Cane Creek to secure the bodies of the murdered elders and send them to Salt Lake.

By the 1890s, most missionaries were young, unmarried men, and by 1898 the first female missionaries were called. Gradually the number of missionaries has grown from about two thousand in the first decade of the twentieth century to more than fifty thousand in the 1990s. More than 2 million copies of the Book of Mormon are published each year in more than fifty languages; many are distributed free.

A typical day for a hard-working missionary and his companion begins at 6:30 A.M. The missionaries, always in twos, study the scriptures and have breakfast. By 9:30 they are out looking for interested people. They knock on doors, talk to people in the streets, and visit members, taking an hour out for lunch and another for dinner. Such serious missionaries are home by 9:30 and in bed by 10:30. Not all are so disciplined, but most try to conform to this pattern.

When asked whether every young man should fill a mission, then-president Spencer W. Kimball answered, "Yes. Every young man should fill a mission." Not every young man does, but the numbers steadily

In 1990, there were more than 40,000 LDS missionaries serving worldwide. Missionaries are not always as well received as those pictured here.

This depiction of a Latter-day Saint's baptism is painted with oils on glass, a technique used in Eastern Europe. The LDS church museum exhibits art from all over the world.

increase. These young men leave college programs, jobs, and serious romances at age nineteen for two years. Mormon missionaries teach the people they meet about the nature of God and the plan of salvation, asking them to repent and be baptized by those holding proper authority. These missionaries are often turned down. Their two mission years are not in fact very efficient in converting new members but the group is so large that convert baptisms between 1986 and 1990 outnumbered baptisms of member children by three to one.

Stewart Carlsen, on a mission to Korea, would set up a display in front of the local train station and try to talk to people about the church.

When someone showed interest, he arranged a home appointment. Stewart found it exciting when the church really helped someone change his or her life. "Working that hard to try to get people interested made me that much more devoted to the church and to the gospel," he recalled.

Robert Hansen loved having only one thing to do for two whole years: serve the Lord "through whatever means were available." He put all his energy and thought into it, learning to get along with people, discovering a talent for organization, and developing close relationships. "You might disagree or be angry at your companion for the things he does, but you can still love him and work together for a common goal."

Ned Orton joined his high school girlfriend's church. He decided to go on a mission only when she said she would not marry him unless he did. He worked and saved for a year, then actually began his mission on the day his girlfriend married someone else. He returned a "totally different person," having learned "as much from the discussions as the people [he] taught." He considered his mission the "whole foundation of [his] life. . . . Even when times have been bad, I've known that the church is true."

Mission work demands extraordinary effort, but the experience provides spiritual enlightenment, lasting friendships, and deep satisfactions. Parents support their missionaries through current income or savings. Some missionaries have bad experiences and return early, but most complete their assignments.

The growth of the church has come about largely because of an energetic missionary program, which included more than 7,000 women in 1990.

The Book of the Mormon Account of the Coming of Jesus Christ to the New World, around 34 A.D.

The prophets in the Book of Mormon foretold the coming of Christ even more specifically than the Old Testament prophets. They said he would be born a woman from Nazareth and go about teaching with Twelve Apostles. They also prophesied his coming to America, following his death and resurrection in Jerusalem.

At the time of the crucifixion, storms and earthquakes devastated Book of Mormon cities, destroying buildings and killing much of the population. As the turmoil abated, the people heard a voice speaking to them out of the heavens, and they know the predicted visit of Christ was about to occur

1. And now it came to pass that there were a great multitude gathered together, of the people of Nephi, round about the temple which was in the land Bountiful; and they were marveling and wondering with one another, and were showing one to another the great and marvelous change which had taken place.

2. And they were also conversing about this Jesus Christ, of whom the sign had been given concerning his death.

3. And is came to pass that while they were thus conversing one with another, they heard a voice as if it came out of heaven; and they cast their eyes around about, for they understood not the voice which they heard; and it was not a harsh voice, neither was it a loud voice; nevertheless, and notwithstanding it being a small voiced it did pierce them that did hear to the center, insomuch that there was no part of their frame that it did not cause to quake; yea, it did pierce them to the very soul, and did cause their hearts to burn.

4. And it came to pass that again they heard the voice, and they understood it not.

5. And again the third time they did hear the voice, and did open their ears to hear it; and their eyes were towards the sound thereof; and they did look steadfastly towards heaven, from whence the sound came.

6. And behold, the third time they did understand the voice which they heard; and it said unto them:

7. Behold my Beloved Son, in whom I am well pleased, in whom I have glorified my name—hear ye him.

8. And it came to pass, as they understood they cast their eyes up again towards heaven; and behold they saw a Man descending out of heaven; and he was clothed in a white robe; and he came down and stood in the midst of them; and the eyes of the whole multitude were turned upon him, and they durst not open their mouths, even one to another, and wist not what it meant for they thought it was an angel that had appeared unto them.

9. And it came to pass that he stretched forth his hand and spake unto the people, saying:

10. Behold, I am Jesus Christ whom the prophets testified shall come into the world.

11. And behold, I am the Light and the life of the world; and I have drunk out of that bitter cup which the Father hath given me, and have glorified with the Father in taking upon me the sins of the world, in the which I have suffered the will of the Father in all things from the beginning.

12. And it came to pass that when Jesus had spoken these words the whole multitude fell to the earth; for they remembered that it had been prophesied among them that Christ should show himself unto them after his ascension into heaven.

—*The Book of Mormon, 3 Nephi 11:1-12*

On June 9, 1978, President Spencer W. Kimball announced that the day had come "when every faithful, worthy man in the Church may receive the holy priesthood," ending the ban on blacks entering the Mormon priesthood.

Increasing numbers of young women choose to go on missions. They feel less pressure to go as they are encouraged to marry instead, and they do not begin missions until age twenty-one. These young people transfer their youthful energies to spreading the gospel, often converting themselves to a deeper faith and commitment as they do.

The missionaries usually make a deep impression on the people they teach. Jean Morton tried to ignore the young men teaching her children, but before she knew it she herself was scheduled for baptism. "I liked the good clean living. I liked the missionaries." She saw that "this is the way I'd like my boys and girls to be."

Others are won over by the Mormon congregations. Valerie Lord, who had problems at home, visited one church as a teenager. There she was impressed by "how friendly everybody was. I'd like to think I joined because I had a testimony, but would I have had a testimony if I hadn't had such a warm reception?"

When Charles Wilson studied the gospel, he prayed to know if the Book of Mormon was a true book. He thought that Mormonism "*should* be true," because it was attractive and compelling, but he wanted to believe. Conversion came to him suddenly. "I merely surrendered as the honest and honorable thing to do."

Not everyone who listens to the missionaries joins this demanding church. When Willis Lincoln was teaching missionary lessons to a family he knew, one night they decided against going any further. "We see how active you are, and that's not for us." He silently agreed that he felt burned out himself.

At one time, missionaries did not in fact encourage everyone to join the church. For many years, church policy withheld the priesthood from blacks "of African lineage," although priesthood authority was routinely bestowed on other young males at age twelve. This controversial policy caused tension and sorrow, as many members believed that it arose out of a historical tradition rather than from inspired revelation. During the civil rights movement of the 1960s, this concern was especially strong. Several thousand faithful black members had joined the church, to be confronted by an official statement of 1969 that read, "Negroes [are] not yet to receive the priesthood, for reasons which we believe are known to God, but which He has not made fully known to man." Mormons believed in the brotherhood of man and were convinced that the gospel was intended for all of God's children. This priesthood ban against blacks seemed to make no sense when the gospel was to be preached to "every nation, kindred, tongue, and people."

On June 9, 1978, President Spencer W. Kimball announced that the day had come "when every faithful, worthy man in the Church may receive the holy priesthood." His announcement, now included in the Doctrine and Covenants, noted that the revelation had resulted from long and earnest prayer. News of the change brought celebration throughout the church as black members immediately prepared for ordination.

In the early years, the converts came primarily from England, Scandinavia, and Germany. In the 1950s, however, growth surged in the Pacific—the Hawaiian Islands, Tonga, the Philippines, and New Zealand. Then the 1960s began to see growth in Latin America and Asia. In the 1970s, an average of one new ward chapel was dedicated somewhere in the world every day. In 1990 one of every five members spoke native Spanish or Portuguese. Recently, missions have opened in the old Eastern bloc countries of the former Soviet Union and in Africa. In the past, immigrants flocked to Zion, joining existing wards that were acculturated to North American norms. Now multiple Zions rise far away from American culture.

The major challenge to the church in the late twentieth century has been this immense international growth. Although it is uniquely American and the largest church founded in the United States, Mormonism is growing most rapidly abroad.

In 1947 the church population was about 1 million. By 1990 the number was over 7 million, reaching 10 million during 1997. In 1950,

The artist of this picture cloth, a convert to the church living in the West African nation of Sierra Leone, depicts how Latter-day Saints in his native land have become self-reliant through hard work.

fewer than 8 percent of Mormons lived outside the United States and Canada. By 1990 the number was more like 35 percent. In 1996 more than half the church's members lived outside the United States, and most of them did not speak English. At the end of 1994, the church had organized groups in 149 nations and territories. Church leaders struggle to sift out the church's Americanisms from its basic teachings. President Joseph Fielding Smith, holding a conference in Manchester, England, in the early 1970s, reminded the members there that the church was an American church only in America. "In Canada it is a Canadian church; in Australia it is an Australian church; and in Great Britain it is a British church. It is a world church; the gospel is for all men."

Cultural conflicts unfortunately occur in nations where brash American teenagers with poor language skills teach the gospel. A missionary to Peru, Linda Hansen, in carrying out the church program, somehow found herself teaching the foxtrot to the remnants of the Inca civilization. Mexican converts have been offended by Mormon artistic interpretations of their culture that they consider ignorant and insulting. Now, however, they interpret Mormon themes in their own way. Such tensions remind LDS leaders that the limitations of nationalism must be resolved to create an international Mormonism.

Another area of cultural conflict has been with Native Americans in the United States. The native population of Mormon country in 1847 has been estimated at about eighteen thousand. But the first systematic count in 1890 yielded only thirty-five hundred. Brigham Young sought to convert and "civilize" the native people, but these positive intentions served to reduce their numbers. Many Native Americans have joined the church, but others have resisted, distrusting Mormons as being Euro-Americans.

In the 1950s the Indian Student Placement Program of the church sought to help young people gain better educations. The dropout rate from federal government boarding schools and schools on reservations

Mormon missionaries baptize Shivwitz Indians in the Southwest in the early 1900s. Many Native Americans have joined the church, but others have resisted, distrusting Mormons as being Euro-Americans.

was then high. Because of the church's special concern for Native Americans, a grassroots program invited native children into Mormon homes for the school year. Families carried the program informally from the late 1940s on, and the church adopted it formally in 1954. In this voluntary program, a foster family provided transportation, food, clothing, and covered school costs. In 1956, 242 students were enrolled in the program. By 1966 there were 1,569 young people from 64 tribes in many states and Canada.

Lance Hoskins, a Native American social worker, joined the Wilson family while in high school, adjusting to three foster siblings and moving on with this military family to several different states, even though the mother later told him, "Lance, that first year with you was pure hell." He attended Brigham Young University and served a two-year Mormon mission term. He has always been aware of cultural tensions between Indian and Anglo Mormons but, nevertheless accepts the teachings of the LDS while clinging to his Native American ways.

Some observers complained that this program broke up Native American families, depriving parents of responsibility for their children. Others feared that the church was using the program for missionary purposes. While the participants had additional educational opportunities and many families and foster children have remained close, the church discontinued the program, because Native Americans were becoming alienated from their own culture. Mormons have since tried to help Native Americans in other ways, but not always successfully.

The effort to include Native Americans in their lives typifies the much broader program of inclusion evident now in Mormon wards everywhere. Members of the church live and work closely with others quite unlike themselves. They must love and serve people they would ordinarily never know. In return for this service, Mormons always have a community, a set of friends available to them in new and unfamiliar places. Whatever the need, Mormons can call upon other church members for help. Because they share common beliefs, behavior, and traditions, otherwise disparate people can become mutually helpful friends almost immediately.

Mormons recognize that their beliefs may seem strange to an unbelieving world. They sometimes feel separated from others because of their unusual teachings. Part of the explanation is of course that people educated in a rational, scientific tradition are often particularly alienated by a religion encompassing ritual and strong faith in divine influence. But the Mormon beliefs are the foundation of the church, providing a sense of meaning and purpose in life that are often missing in the modern world, as well as a perspective within which to answer questions and deal with suffering.

The Latter-day Saints, a modern people in a modern church, still think of themselves as members of the kingdom of God, going forth to preach to all people and prepare the world for the return of Christ. The prospect of the church now is far different than when it began, for it has gained influence far beyond any conceivable expectations at its founding. At its current rate of growth, the Church of Jesus Christ of Latter-day Saints will be a major world religion in the coming century, carrying forward the Mormon Christianity of an earlier time into a fast-changing, challenging future.

The Washington, D.C., temple in Kensington, Maryland.

Chronology

1805
Joseph Smith, Jr., born in Sharon, Windsor County, Vermont, on December 23

1820
Joseph Smith's first vision

1823
Visit of Moroni to Joseph Smith

1827
Joseph Smith obtains plates of the Book of Mormon

1830
Book of Mormon published; Church of Christ organized

1831
Joseph Smith and his followers move to Kirtland, Ohio area; Independence, Missouri (Jackson County), designated as Zion

1833
Mormons driven from Jackson County, Missouri

1836
Temple dedicated in Kirtland, Ohio

1837
Missionary work begun in England

1838
Mormons leave Kirtland area for Far West, Missouri; Mormon War in Missouri; Joseph Smith imprisoned

1839
Mormons move to Nauvoo, Illinois

1842
Female Relief Society organized

1843
Revelation on celestial (plural) marriage recorded

1844
Joseph Smith runs for president of the United States; Smith is assassinated; Brigham Young and Twelve Apostles accepted as leaders of the church

1846
Mormons leave Nauvoo for the West

1847
First Mormon companies arrive in Salt Lake Valley; Brigham Young becomes president of the church

1849
Gold rush immigrants pass through Salt Lake

1850
Brigham Young appointed governor of territory of Utah

1852
Doctrine of plural marriage formally announced

1853
Cornerstone of Salt Lake temple laid

1856
First handcart companies formed

1857
U.S. Army ordered to Utah; massacre of Fancher Party at Mountain Meadows

1858
U.S. army under General Johnston enters Salt Lake Valley

1862
Morrill Anti-Bigamy Act defines plural marriage as a crime with severe penalties

1867
Female Relief Society organization revived and reorganized

1869
Church cooperatives organized; transcontinental railroad completed, ending the pioneer period; Young Ladies Retrenchment Association organized

1870
Mass meeting of Mormon women protests anti-Mormon legislation in Congress; Utah legislature grants women the vote

1872
First issue of *The Woman's Exponent*

1875
Young Men's Mutual Improvement Association organized; Brigham Young Academy founded in Provo

1877
Brigham Young dies

1878
Primary organization for children founded

1879
Supreme Court upholds the Morrill Act of 1862

1880
Jubilee year of celebration and forgiveness of debts; John Taylor sustained as president of the church

1882
Edmunds Anti-Polygamy Act disenfranchises people living in plural marriages

1885
Mormon polygamists go into hiding in the underground

1887
Edmunds-Tucker Act amends and enforces Morrill Anti-Bigamy Act of 1862, disincorporating the church and escheating to the federal government all its property in excess of $50,000; President John Taylor dies

1889

Wilford Woodruff sustained as president of the church, declares an end to the practice of plural marriage

1893

President Benjamin Harrison grants amnesty to polygamists

1896

Utah granted statehood

1898

Wilford Woodruff dies; Lorenzo Snow sustained as president

1899

President Snow emphasizes tithing to help pay church debts

1901

President Snow dies; Joseph Fielding Smith sustained as president

1904

President Smith reemphasizes the ban on plural marriage

1907

Reed Smoot, an Apostle, seated in the Senate after extensive hearings

1918

President Smith receives a revelation on the salvation of the dead; Smith dies; Heber J. Grant sustained as president

1929

Tabernacle Choir begins weekly radio broadcasts

1936

Formal organization of church welfare program

1937

Hill Cumorah pageant begun

1940s

Missionaries work only in North and South America due to World War II; Genealogical Society begins microfilming records worldwide

1945

President Heber J. Grant dies; George Albert Smith sustained as president

1946

President Smith travels to Mexico, the first church president to do so

1947

Celebration of 100 years in the Salt Lake Valley

1950

Early morning seminary for high school students inaugurated

1951

President Smith dies; David O. McKay sustained as president

1954

Church establishes a college in Hawaii; beginning of Indian placement program

1955

First European temple, in Bern, Switzerland, dedicated

1958

New Zealand and London temples dedicated

1961

Correlation Council to coordinate
church programs introduced

1963

Vaults for storage of genealogical
records completed

1965

Home evening program formally
inaugurated

1966

First South American Stake organized in São Paulo, Brazil

1970

President David O. McKay dies;
Joseph F. Smith sustained as president; first stake organized in Asia
in Tokyo, Japan

1971

Medical missionary program
begins

1972

President Smith dies; Harold B.
Lee sustained as president

1973

President Lee dies; Spencer W.
Kimball sustained as president

1975

Church divests itself of 15 hospitals
to be run by non-profit, non-
church organization

1975

Church opens 28 story office
building in Salt Lake City

1976

Church reaffirms policy against
abortion

1978

President Kimball announces
that all worthy men, including
African Americans, to receive
the priesthood

1979

Church's 1,000th stake organized
at Nauvoo, Illinois

1982

Church membership reaches
5,000,000

1985

President Kimball dies; Ezra Taft
Benson sustained as president

1987

Tabernacle Choir marks 3,000th
broadcast

1989

Brigham Young University Center
in Jerusalem dedicated

1994

President Benson dies; Howard W.
Hunter sustained as president

1995

President Hunter dies; Gordon B.
Hinckley sustained as president

1997

Membership exceeds 10,000,000
with more than half outside the
United States

1997

Church reenacts 150th anniversary
of westward pioneer trek

Further Reading

GENERAL READING ON RELIGION IN THE UNITED STATES

Ahlstrom, Sidney. *A Religious History of the American People.* New Haven, Conn.: Yale University Press, 1972.

Butler, Jon, and Harry S. Stout, eds. *Religion in American History: A Reader.* New York: Oxford University Press, 1997.

Gaustad, Edwin S. *A Religious History of America.* Rev. ed. San Francisco: Harper & Row, 1990.

Marty, Martin. *Pilgrims in Their Own Land: 500 Years of Religion in America.* New York: Penguin, 1985.

PRIMARY SOURCES

The Book of Mormon. Salt Lake City, Utah: The Church of Jesus Christ of Latter-day Saints, 1981.

The Doctrine and Covenants. Salt Lake City, Utah: The Church of Jesus Christ of Latter-day Saints, 1981.

History of the Church of Jesus Christ of Latter-day Saints, 7 volumes, introduction and notes by B. H. Roberts. Salt Lake City, Utah: Deseret News, 1952.

The Holy Bible Containing the Old and New Testaments. Salt Lake City, Utah: The Church of Jesus Christ of Latter-day Saints, 1979.

The Pearl of Great Price. Salt Lake City, Utah: The Church of Jesus Christ of Latter-day Saints, 1981.

Smith, Joseph Jr., *The Papers of Joseph Smith*, 2 volumes, ed. Dean C. Jessee. Salt Lake City, Utah: Deseret Book Co., 1989.

Woman's Exponent. Salt Lake City, Utah, 1872–1914.

GENERAL HISTORIES OF THE CHURCH OF JESUS CHRIST OF LATTER-DAY SAINTS

Allen, James B., and Glen M. Leonard. *The Story of the Latter-day Saints.* Salt Lake City, Utah: Deseret Book Co., 1976.

Arrington, Leonard J., and Davis Bitton. *The Mormon Experience: A History of the Latter-day Saints.* New York: Alfred A. Knopf, 1979.

Davis, Inex Smith. *The Story of the Church.* Independence, Mo.: Herald Publishing House, 1948.

Ludlow, Daniel H., ed. *Encyclopedia of Mormonism: The History, Scripture, Doctrine, and Procedures of The Church of Jesus Christ of Latter-day Saints.* New York: Macmillan, 1992.

O'Dea, Thomas F. *The Mormons.* Chicago: University of Chicago Press, 1957.

Shipps, Jan. Mormonism: *The Story of a New Religious Tradition.* Urbana: University of Illinois Press, 1985.

SPECIALIZED TOPICS

Alexander, Thomas G. *Mormonism in Transition: A History of the Latter-day Saints, 1890–1930.* Urbana: University of Illinois Press, 1986.

————— . *Things in Heaven and Earth: The Life and Times of Wilford Woodruff, a Mormon Prophet.* Salt Lake City, Utah: Signature Books, 1991.

Allen, James B. *Trials of Discipleship: The Story of William Clayton, A Mormon.* Urbana: University of Illinois Press, 1987.

Allen, James B., and Richard Cowan. *Mormonism in the Twentieth Century.* 2nd ed. Provo, Utah: Brigham Young University Press, 1967.

Arrington, Leonard J. *Brigham Young: American Moses.* New York: Alfred A. Knopf, 1985.

————— . *Great Basin Kingdom: An Economic History of the Latter-day Saints, 1830–1900.* Cambridge, Mass.: Harvard University Press, 1958.

Arrington, Leonard J., Feramorz Y. Fox, and Dean L. May. *Building the City of God: Community and Cooperation Among the Mormons.* 2nd ed. Urbana: University of Illinois Press, 1992.

Backman, Milton R. *American Religions and the Rise of Mormonism.* Salt Lake City, Utah: Deseret Book Co., 1965.

—————. *The Heavens Resound: A History of the Latter-day Saints in Ohio, 1830–1838.* Salt Lake City, Utah: Deseret Book Co., 1983.

Barlow, Philip L. *Mormons and the Bible: The Place of the Latter-day Saints in American Religion.* New York: Oxford University Press, 1991.

Beecher, Maureen Ursenbach, and Lavina Fielding Anderson. *Sisters in Spirit: Mormon Women in Historical and Cultural Perspective.* Urbana: University of Illinois Press, 1987.

Brodie, Fawn. *No Man Knows My History: The Life of Joseph Smith, the Mormon Prophet.* New York: Alfred A. Knopf, 1945.

Brooks, Juanita. *The Mountain Meadow Massacre.* Stanford, Calif.: Stanford University Press, 1950.

Bushman, Claudia L., ed. *Mormon Sisters: Women in Early Utah.* Cambridge, Mass.: Emmeline Press, 1976.

Bushman, Richard L. *Joseph Smith and the Beginnings of Mormonism.* Urbana: University of Illinois Press, 1984.

Embry, Jessie L. *Mormon Polygamous Families: Life in the Principle.* Salt Lake City: University of Utah Press, 1987.

Fife, Alta, and Austin Fife. *Saints of Sage and Saddle: Folklore Among the Mormons.* Bloomington: University of Indiana Press, 1956.

Firmage, Edwin Brown, and Richard Collin Mangrum. *Zion in the Courts: A Legal History of the Church of Jesus Christ of Latter-day Saints, 1830–1900.* Urbana: University of Illinois Press, 1988.

Flanders, Robert Bruce. *Nauvoo: Kingdom on the Mississippi.* Urbana: University of Illinois Press, 1965.

Foster, Lawrence. *Women, Family, and Utopia: Communal Experiments of the Shakers, the Oneida Community, and the Mormons.* Syracuse, N.Y.: Syracuse University Press, 1991.

Furness, Norman F. *The Mormon Conflict, 1850–1859.* New Haven, Conn.: Yale University Press, 1960.

Hamilton, C. Mark. *Nineteenth-Century Mormon Architecture and City Planning.* New York: Oxford University Press, 1995.

Hansen, Klaus. *Quest for Empire: The Political Kingdom of God and the Council of Fifty in Mormon History.* East Lansing: Michigan State University Press, 1970.

Hardy, B. Carman. *Solemn Covenant: The Mormon Polygamous Passage.* Urbana: University of Illinois Press, 1992.

Hill, Donna. *Joseph Smith, the First Mormon.* Garden City, N.Y.: Doubleday, 1977.

Hill, Marvin S. *Quest for Refuge: The Mormon Flight from American Pluralism.* Salt Lake City, Utah: Signature Books, 1989.

Kimball, Edward L., and Andrew E. Kimball, Jr. *Spencer W. Kimball: Twelfth President of The Church of Jesus Christ of Latter-day Saints.* Salt Lake City, Utah: Deseret Press, 1977.

Larson, Gustive O. *Prelude to the Kingdom: Mormon Desert Conquest. A Chapter in American Cooperative Experience.* Francestown, N.H.: M. Jones Co., 1947.

Launius, Roger D. *Joseph Smith III: Pragmatic Prophet.* Urbana: University of Illinois Press, 1988.

McMurrin, Sterling M. *The Philosophical Foundations of Mormon Theology.* Salt Lake City: University of Utah Press, 1959.

——— . *The Theological Foundations of the Mormon Religion.* Salt Lake City: University of Utah Press, 1965.

Mauss, Armand L. *The Angel and the Beehive: The Mormon Struggle with Assimilation.* Urbana: University of Illinois Press, 1994.

Mulder, William. *Homeward to Zion.* Minneapolis: University of Minnesota Press, 1957.

Nelson, Lowry. *The Mormon Village: A Study in Social Origins.* Salt Lake City: University of Utah Press, 1952.

Newell, Linda King, and Valeen Tippets Avery. *Mormon Enigma: Emma Hale Smith: Prophet's Wife, "Elect Lady," Polygamy's Foe, 1804–1879.* Garden City, N.Y.: Doubleday, 1984.

Peterson, Charles S. *Utah: A Bicentennial History.* New York: Norton, 1977.

Quinn, D. Michael. *Early Mormonism and the Magic World View.* Salt Lake City, Utah: Signature Books, 1987.

Stegner, Wallace. *The Gathering of Zion: The Story of the Mormon Trail.* New York: McGraw-Hill, 1964.

Taber, Susan B. *Mormon Lives: A Year in the Elkton Ward.* Urbana: University of Illinois Press, 1993.

Taylor, P. A. M. *Expectations Westward: The Mormons and the Emigration of Their British Converts in the Nineteenth Century.* Edinburgh: Oliver & Boyd, 1965.

Van Wagoner, Richard S. *Mormon Polygamy: A History.* 2nd ed. Salt Lake City, Utah: Signature Books, 1989.

Index

References to illustrations are indicated by page numbers in italics

Aaron (brother of Moses), 30
Abraham, 120
Africa, *128*
African Americans, 32, 126–27
Alberta, Canada, 105
Americanisms and missionary effort, 128
American Woman Suffrage Association (AWSA), 91
Anthony, Susan B. (national suffrage leader), *91*, 92
Articles of Faith, 48–49, 120
Asia, 127
Attacks against Mormons, 32–35, 39–41, 46–47, 50–51, 53, 55, 76–79, 120
Attacks by Mormons, 77–78
Authority controversy, 30

Bancroft, H. H. (historian), 67
Baptism, *122*
Baptism for the dead, 44, 100, 108–9
Baptists, 12
Basic beliefs of Mormon church, 48–49, 131
Beds, homemade, 70
Bible, 12, 19, 20, 49, 119
Big Horn Basin, Wyoming, 105
Birth rates, 116–17
Blacks, 32, 126–27
Boggs, Lilburn (Missouri governor), *40*, 46
Book of Mormon, 14, 17–22, *18*, 25, 48, *118, 119,* 121, 124–25
Brigham Young University, 107, *108*, 130
Brooklyn (ship for sea voyage), 61
Buchanan, James (U.S. president), 76–77, 79
Bulkley, Newman, 60
Burr, John Atlantic, 61

California Gold Rush (1848), 60, 61, 72
Camp of Israel, 57
Canada, 105, 128

Cane Creek, Tennessee, 120
Cannon, Martha Hughes, Dr., *94,* 95
Capitalism, 99–100
Carson City, Nevada, 73
Carthage, Illinois, 50–51, 53–54
Celestial marriage. *See* Plural marriage
Central America, 19, 20
Christianity, 11, 25, 49, 119
Church institutions, 107–10
Church of Jesus Christ of Latter-day Saints (formal name of Mormon church), 11
Church services of Mormons, 71–72
Church–state relationship, 75–76, 77, 102
Church Welfare Plan, 103–04
Civil rights movement, 127
Civil War, 76–77
Claridge, Elizabeth Ann, 73–74, 83
Clayton, Diantha, 58
Clayton, William C., 58
Clothing, 81–82
Cooperative movement, *98,* 99
Council Bluffs, Iowa, 59
Cowdery, Oliver (early church leader), 18, 22, 29, 30, 36
Coyner, John (Presbyterian educator), 91
Crickets, plague of, 71
Crocheron, Augusta Joyce, 87
Crocheron, Caroline Joyce, 61
Cullom Act (1870), 90
Cultural activities, 106–7, 111
Cultural conflicts, 128–29
Cumming, Alfred (governor of Utah Territory), 76, 78–79

Day of Pentecost, 36
Democratic party, 101
Deseret, 74
Deseret Telegraph, 79
Dickens, Charles, 64
Dispersion, 105–6
Divine healing, 85
Divorce, 88, 116
Doctrine and Covenants, The, 12, *28,* 119, 127
Drought in Utah, 75

Eastern bloc nations, 127
Economic depression of 1837, 37
Economic self–sufficiency, 74, 79, 82, *83,* 99, 104
Edmunds Act (1882), 92
Edmunds–Tucker Act (1887), 93
Education, 107, 117
Election fight in Missouri, 40
Elkhorn, Nebraska, 62
Emigration stream, 105
Endowments, 36, 109
England, 42, 64, 67, 74, 96
Eternal marriage, 45, 46. *See also* Polygamy

Family History Program, 110
Family Home Evening, 114
Family life, 113
Fancher company, 77–78
Farming, 69, 70–71, 75
Far West, Missouri, 27, 39
Fast offerings, 103
Fayette, New York, 22
Feminism, 91, 97
Fillmore, Millard (U.S. president), 74
First Presidency (of Mormon church), 30
First wives, 86
Floyd, John B. (U.S. secretary of war), 77
Fort Bridger, Wyoming, 73, 77
Fort Laramie, Wyoming, 62
Fort Supply, Wyoming, 73, 77

Garden Grove, Iowa, 58
Gathering principle, 27–28, 104
Genealogy, 100, 108, 110
Germany, 67
Gift of tongues, 48, 85
Grand Encampment, 59
Grand Salt Lake Temple, 108
Grant, Heber J., 104
Grasshopper plague, 75
Great Basin, 74
Great Britain. *See* England
Great Depression, 103
Great Salt Lake City, 69–70
Griffin, Mary, 85

Hale, Isaac, 16, 17
Handcart movement, *65,* 65–66
Harmony, Pennsylvania, 16, 17, 18
Haun's Mill, Missouri, 40
Hawaiian Islands, 127
Heavens, three kingdoms in, 31
Hell, 31
Home teachers, 117
Horne, Alice Merrill, 95–*96*
Horne, Henry, 63
Horne, Joseph, 70, 74
Horne, Mary Isabella, 62–63, 70
Hymn book, Latter-day Saints, *17*

Immigration, 64–67, 74, 75, 104, 127
Independence, Missouri, *24,* 26, *27,*
    29, 32–35, 37
Indian Student Placement Program,
    129–30
Industry, 74
International growth of church, 127.
    See also Missionaries
Israelites, 19

Jackson County, Missouri, *33*–35, 59
James the Apostle, 29, 30
Jesus Christ, 20, 28–29, 48, 49, 109,
    119, 124–25
John the Apostle, 29, 30
John the Baptist, 29, 30
Johnston, Albert Sidney, *76,* 77
Jones, Mary Jane Done, 86

Kanesville, Iowa, 61
Kimball, Heber C., 120
Kimball, Sarah M., 90
Kimball, Spencer W., 121–22, *126,* 127
Kirtland, Ohio, 22–23, 25, 26, 29,
    35–37
Kirtland Safety Society, *36*–37
Kirtland Temple, *34,* 35–36
Korea, 122–23
Lamanites, 19–20
Las Vegas, Nevada, 73
Latin America, 127
LDS (Latter-day Saints). *See* Church
    of Latter-day Saints (Mormon
    church)
Leadership, succession issue, 52–53

Lemhi, Idaho, 73
Leonard, Abigail (faith healer), 85
Liberty, Missouri, 41
Lincoln, Abraham (U.S. president),
    89–90
Log houses, *42,* 70, *80*
Los Angeles temple, 108

McCune, George W., 105
Manifesto, 95–96
Marriage, 45, 46
Medical training for women, 84–85
Melchizedek (higher priesthood), 30
Membership certificates (for
    Mormons), *45*
Members, numbers of, 127–28
Methodists, 12
Mexican War (1846–48), 59–60, *72*
Midwifery (assisting childbirth), 84
Militia (Mormon), 43, 77, 78
Miracles, *60,* 71, 72, 85
Missionaries (Mormon), 42, 64, 67,
    77, 104, 120–*23, 121, 126,* 128–29
Mississippi River, *59*
Moab, Utah, 73
Montrose, Iowa, 58
Mormon Battalion (Mexican War),
    59–60, *72*
Mormon corridor, 73
Mormon (Nephite general), 20
Mormon Tabernacle Choir, *6*
Moroni (angel), 14, 15, 16, 20, 21
Morrill Anti-Bigamy Act (1862),
    89–90
Moses, 12, 120
Mountain Meadows massacre, 77
Moyle, Oscar W., 95
Mt. Pisgah, Iowa, 58
Muddy, Nevada, *73,* 73–74
Multiple wives, 45–46, 69, 77, 79, 81
Murder of Joseph Smith, 47, 50–53,
    51, 54
Music, 72
Mussner, Amos Milton, 92–93

National Woman Suffrage
    Association (NWSA), 91
Native Americans, 22, 60–61, 63, *75,*
    77–78, *129,* 129–30

Nauvoo Expositor (Mormon newspa-
    per), 47
Nauvoo, Illinois, 27, *38,* 41, *42–43,*
    47, *55,* 58, *60,* 74, 81–82
Nauvoo legion, 77, 93
Nauvoo Temple, 43–*44,* 54–55
Near-famine of 1855–57, 75, 87
Nephi, 19–20, 124
Nephi, Utah, 83
New Jerusalem, 25–26, 69
Newspapers owned by Mormons, 47,
    50
New Testament, 119
New Zealand, 127

Old Testament, 119
Opposition to Mormonism, 89–91,
    92–94

Pacific region, 127
Paiute Indians, *75*
Palmyra, New York, 12, 19, 120
Partridge, Edward, 32
Paul the Apostle, 49, 109
Pearl of Great Price, The, 119, 120
Perkins, David, 101
Perpetual Emigration Fund, 64, 93
Peru, 129
Peter the Apostle, 29, 30, 36
Philippines, 127
Pioneers on westward trek, 57–67
Plan of Salvation, 109
Plates of gold (found by Joseph
    Smith), 14–15, 17, 20, 21–*22*
Plural marriage, 45–46, 69, 77, 79,
    81, 86–95, 102
Political office, 95–96, 101–02
Polygamy, 45–46, 69, 77, 79, 81,
    86–95, 101–2, 102
Presbyterians, 12, 14
President of church, 118–19
Priesthood, 30
"Priesthood of Aaron," 30
Primary Association, 106, 114
Principle, the. *See* Plural marriage
Prison terms for polygamy, 92–93, *93*
Promised Land, 19, 59
Property ownership, 26
Protestant religions, 29–30

Quakers, 12
Quorum of the Twelve Apostles, 30, 41, 52–53, 118–19

Railroads, 67, 79, 91
Red Cross, 102–3
Reform movement of 1855, 75–76
Relief Society, 81–82, *82*, 84, 85, 91, 102–03, 106, 114–15
Relief Society Halls, 82
Religious services, 71–72, 114
Reorganized Church of Jesus Christ of Latter-day Saints, 53
Republican party, 89, 101
Rigdon, Sidney, 22–23, 31, 40, 53
Robbins, Georgiana Pacific, 61
Roberts, B. H. , *101*–02
Roman Catholic church, 30
Roosevelt, Theodore (U.S. president), 102
Roughing It (Twain), 92

Sabbath meetings, 71
Sacrament Meeting, 114, *115*
St. George, Utah, 100
Saints, 26, 27, 32–35
Salt Lake City, Utah, 27, *65*, 69–70, *78*, 85, 99–100, 118
Salt Lake Tabernacle, 90, 100
Salt Lake Temple, *110, 111*
Salt Lake Valley, 62, *63*, 64
San Bernardino, California, 73
Satan, 31
Scandinavia, 64, 67, 96
Schools, 107
Seagulls (miracle of the gulls), *71*
Sea voyage (around South American continent), 61
Second wives, 87
Sericulture (raising silkworms), *83*
Sessions, Patty, 84, 89
Sexuality, 116
Sharon, Vermont, 12
Sharp, Thomas, 47, 50
Shipp, Ellis, 84–85
Sierra Leone, *128*
Silkworms, *83*

Slavery, 32
Smith, Bathsheba, 95
Smith, Emma Hale, *16,* 17, 23, 39, *42,* 45, 53, 82, 87, *88*
Smith, Hyrum, 51, *52*
Smith, Joseph, III, 16, 53
Smith, Joseph F., 104–5
Smith, Joseph Fielding, 128
Smith, Joseph, *10,* 11–23, *13, 42,* 81–82, 85, 86, 87, *88,* 101, 117, 120. *See also* Murder of Joseph Smith
Smith, Joseph, Sr., 12–13, 16
Smith, Lucy Mack, 12–13
Smith, Samuel, 120
Smith, William, 53
Smoot, Reed, *102*
Snow, Eliza R., 82, *87,* 90
Snow, Lorenzo, 100, *104*
Snowstorms, 66
Soldiers, invasion by federal, 76–79
Sorenson, Hannah, 84
Speaking in tongues, 48, 85
Stakes (dioceses), 105, 114
Standing, Joseph, 120
Stansbury, Howard, 71–72
Stanton, Elizabeth Cady, 91
Stenhouse, Fanny, 85
Sunday School program, 106

Teenagers, 117
Temple attendance, 100
Temples built by Mormons, 35–36, 43–44, 108
Ten Tribes (Mormon belief), 48
Testimony meeting, 117
Tithing to the church, 26, 74, 100, 116
Tonga, 127
Toys, *43*
Transportation system (to Utah), 66–67
Twain, Mark, 92
Twelve Apostles, 30, 124. *See also* Quorum of the Twelve Apostles

University of Deseret, 95
U.S. troops, invasion by, 76–79
Utah, 69–79, 107
Utah statehood, *98*
Utah Territory, 74, 89
Utah war, *76*–79, *78*

Van Buren, Martin (U.S. president), 43
Visitations, 29–30
Visiting teachers, 117

Wagon trains, *55, 56,* 57–61, *59, 62*–67, *66*
Wards, 113, 130
Ward bishops, 113–14, 118
Warsaw Signal (Illinois newspaper), 47
Washington, D.C., temple, 108, *131*
Welfare programs, 100, *103*–04, 111
Westward migration, 57–67
Wheat supplies, 84
Whitmer family, 18, 22
Winter Quarters, Nebraska's Indian Territory, 61
Woman's Exponent, 86, 91
Woman suffrage, 81, 90, 91, 94, 95
Women, 30, 81–97, 114–15, 121, 123, 126
Women's groups, 102
Woodruff, Wilford, 94
Word of Wisdom (dietary code), 31, 100, 101
World War I, 102–3

Yerba Buena (now San Francisco), California, 61
Young, Brigham, 41, 42, *53*–54, 57, 62, 66, *68,* 69, 72, 73, 76, *78,* 81, 82, 84, 86, 87, 88, 120, 129
Young, Harriet Decker, 69
Young Women's and Young Men's Mutual Improvement Associations, 106

Zion, 26, 48
Zion of Utah, 105

Acknowledgments

A number of people read the manuscript of this book and offered astute suggestions. Our thanks go to the staff of the Joseph Fielding Smith Institute, especially Carol Madsen and William Hartley, and also to Cherry Silver, an intellectual-at-large on Mormon topics.

Nancy Toff, a veteran editor of books for young people, deserves credit for conceiving of the series along with the editors Jon Butler and Harry Stout, who substantially improved the early drafts. Beth Harrison capably saw the manuscript through the press.

After we completed the manuscript, we realized that among the potential readers were our own grandchildren. Hence the dedication to them.

Picture Credits

© The Church of Jesus Christ of Latter-Day Saints, Courtesy of Museum of Church History and Art, Used by Permission: 6, 10, 17, 18, 28, 34, Nauvoo, Illinois, 1859 by Johannes Schroeder: 38, 40, 45, 49, 53, Martyrdom Sampler by Mary Ann Broomhead: 54, First Glimpse of 'The Valley': 63, The Handcart Family by Torleif Knaphus: 65, 73, Organization of Relief Society in Nauvoo, March 17, 1842: 82, 83, 88, 94, 101, 104, 110, Sesquicentennial Quilt by Oakland Stake Relief Society: 112, 118, 119, Early Morning Baptism Near Belgrade by Ljiljana Crnogaj Fulepp: 122, 126, Becoming Self Reliant by Abu Aassan Conteh: 128, 129; Photographic Archives, Harold B. Lee Library, Brigham Young University, Provo, Utah: 35, 36, 50, 75, 87, 93 (neg. no. 2111); © Courtesy Museum of Art, Brigham Young University, All Rights Reserved: Flight by Minerva Teichert: 21; Saints Driven from Jackson County Missouri by C. C. A. Christensen: 33; The Gulls by Minerva Teichert: 71; Crossing the Mississippi on the Ice by C. C. A. Christensen: 59; Catching Quails by C. C. A. Christensen: 60; Denver Public Library, Western History Collection: 56; Library of Congress: 91; Library-Archives, Reorganized Church of Jesus hrist of Latter Day Saints, Independence, Missouri: 16, 22, 42; Missouri Historical Society, St. Louis: 24, 44, 51; Artist Gary E. Smith: 13; Photo Courtesy State Historical Society of Iowa—Iowa City: 55; Public Communications/Special Affairs Department, The Church of Jesus Christ of Latter-Day Saints: 2, 115, 121, 123, 131; The Pioneer Memorial Museum, International Society Daughters of Utah Pioneers: 43; Utah State Historical Society, All Rights Reserved: 52, 66, 76, 78, 68, 72, 80, 96, 98, 103, 111.

Claudia Lauper Bushman

Claudia Lauper Bushman teaches American studies at Columbia University. She earned an A.B. in English literature from Wellesley College, an M.A. in American literature from Brigham Young University, and a Ph.D. in American studies from Boston University. She is the author of a number of books, including *Mormon Sisters: Women in Early Utah* and *America Discovers Columbus.* She is the founder and first editor of the *Exponent II,* a quarterly newspaper for Mormon women.

Richard Lyman Bushman

Richard L. Bushman is Gouverneur Morris professor of history at Columbia University, and professor at the Bard Graduate Center for Studies in the Decorative Arts. He earned an A.B. from Harvard College, and an A.M. in history and a Ph.D. in the history of American civilization from Harvard University. He is a former Bishop and Stake President of the Church of Jesus Christ of Latter-day Saints, and the author of several books, including *Joseph Smith and the Beginnings of Mormonism* and *The Great Awakening: Documents of the Revival of Religion 1740–1745.*

Jon Butler

Jon Butler is the William Robertson Coe Professor of American Studies and History and Professor of Religious Studies at Yale University. He received his B.A. and Ph.D. in history from the University of Minnesota. He is the coauthor, with Harry S. Stout, of *Religion in American History: A Reader,* and the author of several other books in American religious history including *Awash in a Sea of Faith: Christianizing the American People,* which won the Beveridge Award for the best book in American history from the American Historical Association.

Harry S. Stout

Harry S. Stout is the Jonathan Edwards Professor of American Christianity at Yale University. He is the general editor of the Religion in America series for Oxford University Press and co-editor of *Readings in American Religious History, New Directions in American Religious History, A Jonathan Edwards Reader,* and the *Dictionary of Christianity in America.* His book *The Divine Dramatist: George Whitefield and the Rise of Modern Evangelicalism* was nominated for a Pulitzer Prize in 1991.